LECTURE SERIES Vol. 1

PARABLES OF THELEMA

THE PARABLE OF THE NEW BIRTH

✸

THE PARABLE OF THE PALE IMAGE

✸

THE PARABLE OF THE HUMMINGBIRD

✸

J. Daniel Gunther

WENNOFER HOUSE

Copyright © 2022 J. Daniel Gunther
All rights reserved

All original artwork by Annette Eustace Gray © 2022

No part of this publication may be reproduced or transmitted in any form or by any means, electronic or mechanical, including photocopying, recording or by an information storage and retrieval system, without permission in writing from Wennofer House.
Reviewers may quote brief passages.

ISBN 978-0-9995936-3-9

Cover Art: "The exceeding light" by Annette Eustace Gray

Preface

J Daniel Gunther first lectured on the Parables of Thelema in 2014 e.v. in Sydney, Australia. The following year it was delivered in Austin, Los Angeles and Seattle, and in 2016 in Stockholm (Sweden), Indianapolis and Belgrade (Serbia). Later the lecture was presented in 2017 in London (England), in 2018 in Montreal (Canada) and in 2021, Parables of Thelema received global audiences with two online presentations hosted in Miami and Stockholm (Sweden). The overwhelming majority of these lectures were presented by local or national sections of Ordo Templi Orientis (OTO).

The lecture has now been edited and expanded for print and e-book publication. See the Introduction for details.

Acknowledgments

I give my sincere thanks to Annette Eustace Gray for the design and production of this book which is enlivened by many of her inspired illustrations. The original artwork slides she produced for the original lecture serve as the basis for this publication.

Typesetting of the Demotic and Egyptian and Hieroglyphics was provided by Ian Mercer utilizing the JSesh program, and creating special characters not contained in the standard font set. Brendan Walls proofread and verified the Hieroglyphic texts. Matthew Andrews proofread the manuscript and verified the Greek text. His many contributions to this work were invaluable. Gordan Djurdjevic proofread and verified the Sanskrit entries, offering many useful suggestions. The Hebrew texts were proofread and verified by Marko Milenovic. Proofreadings and verification of the quotes from the Holy Books were provided by Brendan Walls, Dathan Biberstein, Gwen Gunther, Marko Milenovic, Matthieu Kleemann and Santo Rizzuto.

Ian Mercer also drew the color diagrams of The Tree of Life, The Powers of the Sphinx and The Tzelim. The illustration of Hadit was drawn by Jasenka Avram.

The book was edited by Stephen J. King.

All uncredited translations of Egyptian, Greek and

Hebrew are my own and I assume full responsibility for their content.

Lastly, once again, I wish to thank all of the individuals world-wide who requested and sponsored my original lectures, welcoming my wife and myself into their fraternal communities.

J. Daniel Gunther

Abbreviations utilized

777	*777 Revised*
Allen	*Middle Egyptian*, James P. Allen
BD	*The Egyptian Book of the Dead*
BM	The British Museum
CDME	*A Concise Dictionary of Middle Egyptian*, R.O. Faulkner
Crum	*A Coptic Dictionary*, W.E. Crum
Gesenius	*Gesenius' Hebrew and Chaldee Lexicon of the Old Testament Scriptures*
Liber AL	*Liber AL vel Legis sub figurâ CCXX. The Book of the Law.*
Liber VII	*Liber Liberi vel Lapidis Lazuli - sub figurâ VII*
Liber LXV	*Liber Cordis Cincti Serpente - sub figurâ* אדני
LSJ	Liddell-Scott-Jones, *A Greek-English Lexicon* (1968)
OLD	*Oxford Latin Dictionary* (2016)
Skeat	*Concise Etymological Dictionary of the English Language*
Vision & The Voice	*Liber XXX Aerum vel Sæcvli sub figurâ CCCCXVIII*
Vycichl	*Dictionnaire Étymologique de la langue Copte*
Wb	*Wörterbuch der Aegyptischen Sprache*, Adolf Erman and Hermann Grapow

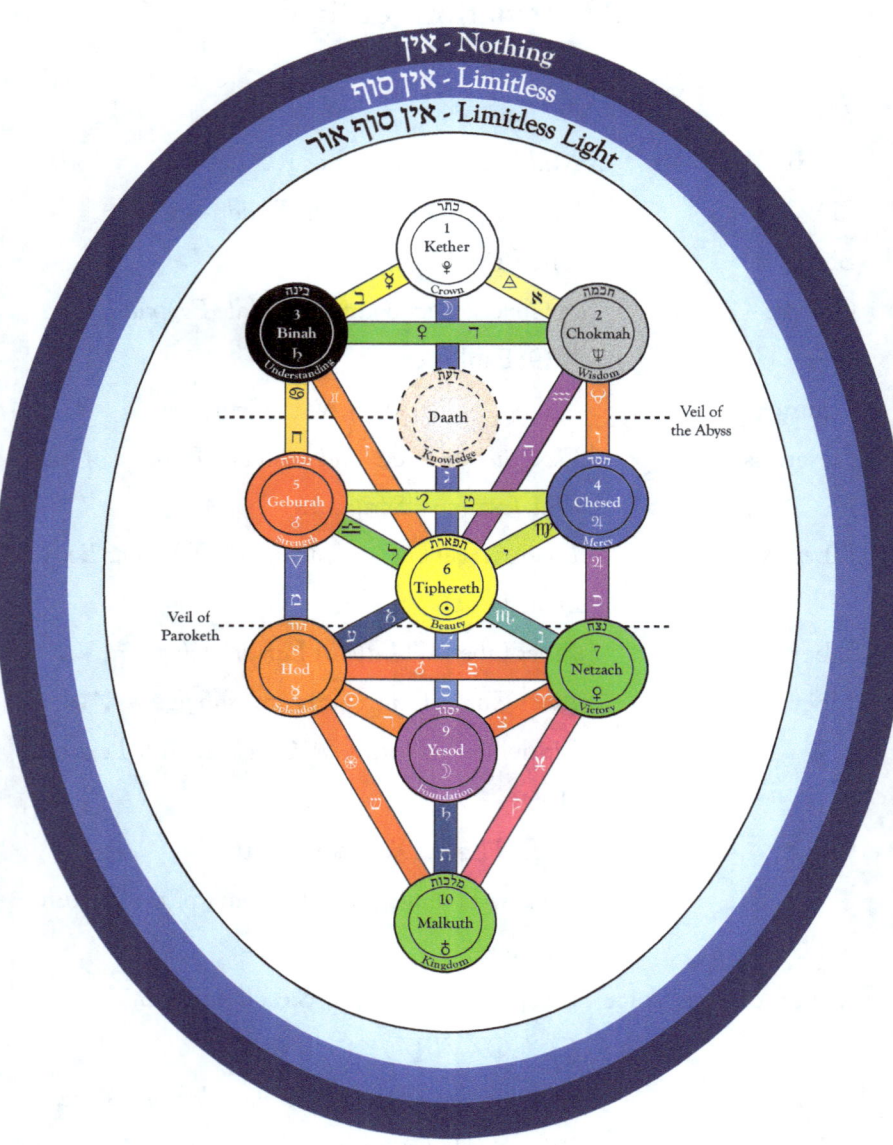

Introduction

Do what thou wilt shall be the whole of the Law.

The Parables of Thelema are taken from a lecture transcript by J. Daniel Gunther. It examined a series of parables found in *Liber LXV, The Book of the Heart Girt with the Serpent*, one of the Holy Books of Thelema. This is now offered in print and e-book by Wennofer House.

The parables are titled with the names given to them by Gunther in the lecture; *Parable of the New Birth, Parable of the Pale Image* and *Parable of the Hummingbird*. The original lecture slide deck has been selectively incorporated into the text, while the published format has allowed for detailed referencing and much additional content. Time and the other constraints of lecturing couldn't accommodate for this important extra information, which is a bonus here. Other than these additions, the lecture is published as it was written and delivered, retaining the cadence and interactivity of Gunther's lecturing style.

Parables are didactic stories of instruction and those of Thelema are no different. They break from the general scriptural narrative into storytelling, imparting valuable lessons to the reader through analogy. In *The Book of the Heart Girt with the Serpent*, these lessons pertain to spiritual

Aspiration. The book is, after all, one of the more personal accounts of the dealing of Initiates with God.

The Parable of the New Birth instructs the Aspirant to abandon the death which the world calls life, in order to embrace the life — the New Birth — which the world calls death. The Parable of the Pale Image is a lesson in overcoming the worship of the Fatal Image of Nature — the Pale Image — in order to worship the essence of God. The Parable of the Hummingbird reminds the Aspirant that in order to experience the precious gifts granted to the Initiate, you must first be an Initiate — not a Hummingbird. You must start at the beginning and endure until the end. While the parables have a special relationship to the initiatic system of the A∴ A∴ and to Thelemites of all persuasions, they speak universally to all spiritual Aspirants.

Most readers would be familiar with the parables of Jesus in the New Testament. Naming the story lessons of *The Book of the Heart Girt with the Serpent* 'parables' in this place, a term that is not used in the Holy Book, might therefore evoke some objection or comparison. In *Parable of the New Birth* Gunther introduces the genre of the parable, its history and qualities, so we know exactly what we are looking at and how to treat these Parables of Thelema. And so far as the New Testament goes, beyond sharing the same method of instruction, any comparison ends there.

According to the New Testament itself, its parables were used specifically for those considered "without", whereas for the disciples of Jesus — those considered "within" — the "mystery of the kingdom of God" was openly "given" (see Mark 4:11). The Parables of the New Aeon are incommensurable with this outlook and approach. They are not "Christian". They do not share the New Testament vision or mission, its doctrine or tenets. They are for all, pointing to methods of Attainment in reach of all who genuinely Aspire to the kingdom of God that is within you.

As a Publication of the A∴A∴ in Class A, *The Book of the Heart Girt with the Serpent* inclusive of its parables is considered beyond rational criticism and is not to be changed. Essential to its understanding are the dramatis personae that are key to its revelation: Adonai, V.V.V.V.V., the Magister, the Adept, the Servant or Scribe. Adonai communicates to the Magister, who instructs the Adept, who may also be called The Servant or The Scribe.

Earlier I skirted around this difficult doctrine saying *The Book of the Heart Girt with the Serpent* is "one of the more personal accounts of the dealing of Initiates with God." The Parables of Thelema and Gunther's exposition of the same, on the other hand, actively explores it. Gunther does so with clarity, empathy, intellectual rigor and authority.

Importantly, Daniel appreciates the beauty of these parables. The Parables of Thelema are to be enjoyed in their beatific simplicity and sublimity.

May this lecture essay bring the reflective Aspirant closer to the joy and beauty of the parables' eternal Truth.

May the A∴ A∴ crown the work, lend us of its wisdom in the work, enable us to understand the work!

Love is the law, love under will.

Fraternally,

Shiva X° (Stephen J. King)
National Grand Master General
Ordo Templi Orientis
Grand Lodge of Australia

LECTURE SERIES Vol. 1

PARABLES OF THELEMA
Part I

THE PARABLE OF THE NEW BIRTH

Liber LXV, Chapter 1, verses 47-48

Title Page Art: Korinna Divergent by Annette Eustace Gray

τὸ γεγεννημένον ἐκ τῆς σαρκὸς σάρξ ἐστιν, καὶ τὸ γεγεννημένον ἐκ τοῦ πνεύματος πνεῦμά ἐστιν.

ΙΩΝΝΗΣ 3:6

List of Illustrations

p. 12	'The Tree of Life,' *Ian Mercer.*
p. 25	'There was a maiden,' *Annette Eustace Gray.*
p. 26	'The Rape of Persephone,' *Simone Pignoni (c. 1650 e.v.)*
p. 28	'The Return of Persephone,' *Lord Frederick Leighton (c, 1891 e.v.)*
p. 32	'strayed,' *Annette Eustace Gray.*
p. 33	'Narcissus,' *John William Waterhouse (1912 e.v.)*
p. 35	'Echo and Narcissus,' *John William Waterhouse (1903 e.v.)*
p. 36	'Inscription in the Temple of Apollo at Delphi, imagined.'
p. 37	'The Death Flower,' *Annette Eustace Gray.*
p. 39	'The Narcissus opening the Gates of Hades,' *Annette Eustace Gray.*
p. 41	'A New Flower,' *Annette Eustace Gray.*
p. 43	'The Rape of Proserpine,' *Joseph Heintz the Elder (1595 e.v.)*
p.44	'Sol Niger' *J. Daniel Gunther, Opus Alchymicum (Black Edition, 2023 e.v.)*
p. 46	'Extraversion,' *Annette Eustace Gray.*

p. 47   'Introversion,' *Annette Eustace Gray*.
p. 48   'Centroversion,' *Annette Eustace Gray*.
p. 51   'Chrysanthemum' *J. Daniel Gunther,*
                   Opus Alchymicum (Black Edition, 2023 e.v.)

PARABLE OF THE NEW BIRTH

At this time, I would like for us to explore one of the Holy Books of Thelema in a very particular way. We are going to use *Liber LXV*, *Liber Cordis Cincti Serpente - sub figurâ* אדני. The name of the book in English is *The Book of the Heart Girt with a Serpent*. We will examine one of the Parables of Thelema. During this lecture, if you want to take notes, I don't mind at all. In fact, I encourage you to do so.

By simplest definition, a Parable is a didactic story which illustrates one or more instructive lessons. A parable is a type of analogy. In fact, the word comes from the Greek παραβολὴ (*parabolē*), which means "comparison, illustration or analogy."[1]

Most of us are familiar with the parables of Jesus in the New Testament — the *Parable of the leaven*, the *Parable of the friend at night*, the *Parable of the good Samaritan* and so on.[2]

Parables have been with us for a very long time; there are examples of parables from ancient Egypt. In the *Berlin Papyrus 3024*, *The Report About the Dispute Between a Man with*

---
1   LSJ 1305b.
2   Parable of the leaven, *Matthew* 13:33-34, Parable of the friend at night, *Luke* 11:5-13, Parable of the good Samaritan, *Luke* 10:29-37.

his Ba-soul, there are some lovely, short parables.[3]

That papyrus dates from the Middle Kingdom, which is between 2000 BCE and 1700 BCE. So you see, they are a very old method of teaching. Parables are effective, in my opinion, because they prompt one to think, and they give the attentive listener a good mnemonic that enables them to remember the moral or point of the parable easily.

So, it should come as no surprise to find them in some of the Holy Books, and in particular, *Liber LXV*, because it is one of the more personal accounts of the dealing of an Initiate with God.

I am going to begin with the first parable in the book. I call it, "The Parable of the New Birth." It is found in *Liber LXV*, Chapter 1, verses 47-48.

47. **There was a maiden that strayed among the corn, and sighed; then grew a new birth, a narcissus, and therein she forgot her sighing and her loneliness.**

48. **Even instantly rode Hades heavily upon her, and ravished her away.**

As we are reading *Liber LXV*, Chapter 1, when we reach verse 47, the Angel dictating the Book abruptly initiates a

---

[3] See James Allen, *The Debate between a Man and His Soul: A Masterpiece of Egyptian Literature*, and Mariam Lichtheim, *Ancient Egyptian Literature, Vol. 1*, "The Dispute Between a Man and His Ba" (pp. 163-169). Raymond Faulkner published his translation in JEA 42 (1956), pp. 21-40, under the title "*The Man Who Was Tired of Life.*"

parable, and the subject of his parable is the Greek goddess *Persephone*.

47. **There was a maiden that strayed among the corn, and sighed; then grew a new birth, a narcissus, and therein she forgot her sighing and her loneliness.**

We know that the maiden who "strayed among the corn" is Persephone, because verse 48, which follows, tells us immediately that the maiden was "ravished away" by *Hades*, the god of the Underworld.

The two characters of Persephone and Hades comprise two of the *dramatis personae* of one of the more well-known myths from ancient Greece, a tale beloved for centuries; a myth that, in its simplest form, explains why there are different seasons in the year.

In the myth, the innocent goddess Persephone is stolen away by Hades, the Lord of Hell. In grief, vegetation begins to die, and soon after, winter comes with its icy chill.

**"Herald of winter's reign,
Persephone is called to the hollow earth.
It is the season of the sombre masque"**[4]

After a series of intrigues, Hades allows Persephone to return to the earth for a time, but she is required to remain under the earth for a third part of the year.[5] When she is

---

4   Gunther, *Northern Cross* (unpublished)

5   *Homeric Hymn II, To Demeter*, 399. The third portion of the year was the winter season. *Pseudo-Apollodorus* confirmed this time period:

returned to the surface, Spring comes with her, followed by the Summer of the year.

The name Persephone is commonly written in Greek as Περσεφόνη. This is the Ionic form of her name in the epic literature.[6] In *The Odyssey*, Homer called her Περσεφονεία

Περσεφόνη δε καθ' ἕκαστον ἐιαυτὸν τὸ μὲν τρίτον μετὰ Πλούτωνος ἠναγκάσθη μένειν, τὸ δὲ λοιπὸν παρὰ τοῖς θεοῖς. "But Persephone was compelled to remain a third of every year with Pluto (i.e. Hades) and the remainder with the gods." (*Bibliotheca* 1,5,3). To ensure that Persephone must return to him, Hades tricked her into eating a pomegranate seed. Hades falsely offered Persephone the freedom to return to her mother upon the earth, "But he stealthily gave her a honeyweet pomegranate seed to eat... so that she might not remain there for all time with the revered, dark-robed Demeter." With hopes for her daughter to be returned to the earth, Demeter asked her, "My child, I do hope you did not taste any food when you were down below? Speak and hide nothing, that we may both know. For if you have not, you can be free from abominable Hades, and live with me and your father..." Persephone answered, "Well then, mother, I will tell you everything truthfully...he stealthily gave me a pomegranate seed, that honeysweet food, and with force he constrained me to taste it against my will." (*Homeric Hymn II, To Demeter*, 370-413, trans. Matthew Andrews). For a magical interpretation of a portion of this myth, see *The Vision and the Voice*, 8th Aethyr.

6   LSJ 1395b. In *Magna Graecia* she was known as Προσερπίνε, *Proserpinē*, from whence the Romans derived her name and legend, calling her *Proserpina*: *Terrena autem vis omnis atque natura Diti patri dedicata est, qui Dives, ut apud Graecos Πλούτων, quia et recidunt omnia in terras et oriuntur e terris. Cui Proserpinam nuptam, quod Graecorum nomen est; ea enim est, quae Περσεφόνη Graece nominatur, quam frugum semen esse volunt absconditamque quaeri a matre fingunt.* "All earthly and natural power is dedicated to Father *Dis*, in Greek Πλούτων, because all things arise from the earth and return to it. To whom *Proserpine* was married, which is a Greek name, for she is the one whom the Greeks call Περσεφόνη), by which they mean the seed of corn, who was hidden, and sought by her Mother." (Cicero, *De Natura Deorum*, 2.26)

(Persephoneia).⁷ In other dialects she was known under other names that were quite different.

In his tragedy Ἀντιγόνη (Antigone), Sophocles called her Φερσέφασσα (Phersephassa).⁸ In his comedy, Βάτραχοι (The Frogs), Aristophanes gave her name as Φερσέφαττα (Phersephatta).⁹ In Cratylus, Plato's character Socrates informs us that her name was Φερρέφαττα (Pherrephatta), incredulously noting that people feared the aspect of that name and therefore changed it to Φερσεφόνη.¹⁰ He then added that Φερέπαφα "or something of that sort, would

---

7   LSJ 1395b. Cf. The Odyssey, Book 11, 47.
8   Sophocles, Antigone, 894.
9   Aristophanes, Ranae, 671.
10 Plato, Cratylus, 404c.

therefore be the correct name of the goddess, because she is wise (σοφίαν) and touches that which is in motion (φερομένου)."[11]

Cratylus is a dialogue about the correctness of names, hence the discussion concerning Persephone. Yet, the discourse concerning this goddess is quite telling in a very specific way other than the fact that her name was surrounded with taboo.[12]

All of these variations of her name suggest to us that the Greeks had difficulty in pronouncing her original name. No doubt, this was because her original name had a pre-Greek origin, from the time *before* Proto-Greek speakers occupied that region. It is a very ancient name with roots in pre-history.[13] In other words, her proper name very probably originated during the period that we call the Aeon of Isis. Is that important? Yes. But I'm going to leave it to you to think about *why* for a moment.

To continue, we note that Xenophon, in the 6th book of his *History of Greece*, referred to her by the name of Κόρη

---

11 *Ibid.*

12 In Euripides' *Helena*, 1307, she is called, ἀρρήτου κούρας, "the maiden (*Korē*) whom none may name." In Homer, *Iliad* 9.457, she is called ἐπαινὴ Περσεφόνεια, "dread Persephone."

13 Chadwick, *The Mycenaean World*, pp. 95 ff. In the *Linear B* script of Mycenaean Greek, the names of *Persephone* and *Kore* have been proposed for 𐀟𐀩𐀲 ("pe-re-swa") and 𐀒𐀷 ("ko-wa"). This proposal continues to be debated. Linear B predates the Greek alphabet by several centuries, the oldest example being ca. 1450 BCE.

(Korē).¹⁴ Now, this last name is important to us, because it literally means "maiden,"¹⁵ as in the "maiden who strayed among the corn." It confirms for us, yet again, that this verse, without a doubt, is speaking about Persephone.

I want you all to note something very interesting here. I mentioned earlier that the name Korē as a substitute for Persephone came about because uttering the name Persephone, in this and all its variants, was *taboo*. She was the consort of Hades, and therefore she was considered the terrible Queen of the Dead. Thus, people began to refer to her euphemistically as Korē, "the maiden," because it wasn't considered safe to utter her real name. We can understand that taboo in the context of superstitions from the ancient past. But why is that interesting to us today?

The name of Persephone does not appear in these verses does it? She is only called "the maiden," Korē. Does the absence of the name in this place represent a taboo? Or does it point us in another direction?

47. **There was a maiden that strayed among the corn, and sighed; then grew a new birth, a narcissus, and therein she forgot her sighing and her loneliness.**

Persephone, or Korē the maiden, symbolizes the

---

14 *Xenophontis Historia Graeca*, VI, 3, 6.
15 *LSJ* 980b.

"earth-bound soul," that is to say, one who does not aspire to the Spiritual Life. She represents the part of the Soul, that in one sense, we call the נפש, *Nephesh*, the so-called "animal soul" or the instincts.

The verse tells us that she "strayed among the corn." Here is the key word to understanding this verse. That word is "strayed."

"There was a maiden that *strayed* among the corn."

To *stray* means to *wander*,[16] that is, to go beyond some established limit. It means to go somewhere *you are not supposed to go*. It is connected to our word **astray** — off of the desired or correct path — in her case, the path that she had followed since when? Since the *Aeon of Isis*. Aha! There we are.

Remember what I asked you to think about? Her name originated in the Aeon of Isis. For millennia she had a proper place, a proper way to behave — all formed during the Aeon of the Mother. But now we see that Persephone had *strayed*.

---

16   Skeat, *Concise Etymological Dictionary of the English Language* (Oxford, 1885) p. 472b.

"There was a maiden that strayed among the corn."

You see, the corn was the domain of Persephone's Mother *Demeter* (Δημήτηρ), the Queen of the bountiful harvest.[17] Persephone was the goddess of innocence, but now she *strayed* into the fields of her Mother. Archetypally, that tells us that she was attempting to abandon childhood and become a woman — to take the place of the Mother. Note that *Liber LXV* says explicitly that she "grew a new birth."

---

17   One of her Epithets was Σιτώ, "she of the grain". (Aelian, *Varia Historia*, 1.27 Cf. *Eustathius of Thessalonica, Scholia on Homer's Iliad*, 265, 30).

Here we are reminded of the Greek word νεόφυτος, neophyte — "newly planted."[18] The Neophyte begins to grow a new birth, like a new plant.

This Holy Book tells us that her new birth was that of a *Narcissus* flower.[19] Becoming the Narcissus, she forgot her

---

18   *LSJ* p. 1170a.

19   The narcissus was the specific flower associated with Persephone and Demeter. "The narcissus blooms daily with its fair clusters; it is the ancient crown of the Great Goddesses." (Sophocles, *Œdipus Coloneus*, 683)

sighing and loneliness, which was her former condition of isolation and despair — the condition of the exiled שכינה, *Shekinah*, the soul cut off from union with God.[20] The details of the Greek myth recount how Persephone was bending down to pick a Narcissus when she was abducted by Hades.[21]

We all remember the myth of *Narcissus* do we not? He was a youth who rejected all those who sought his love.

---

20   שכינה, *Shekinah*, "indwelling", derives from שכן, "to dwell, rest". In post-biblical texts it came to signify the Divine Presence. (Jastrow, *A Dictionary of the Targumim, The Talmud Babli and Yerushalmi, and the Midrashic Literature*, Vol. 2, p.198b.) Qabalists identified the *Shekinah* with *Heh Final* of *Tetragrammaton*, attributed to *Malkuth*, the tenth Sephira on the Tree of Life and the Bride of God. With the destruction of the Temple in Jerusalem and the subsequent Babylonian exile there arose the doctrine of *Shekinah* abandoning God to go with her children into exile until the Temple be rebuilt. It thus symbolizes the Soul cut off from the Divine Presence, that is to say, one who has not attained to the Knowledge and Conversation of the Holy Guardian Angel.

21   Briefly mentioned by Hesiod in his *Theogony*, 913-914 and at greater length in the *Homeric Hymn to Demeter*. According to Pausanias, the Athenian poet Pamphos said, "the Maid, the daughter of Demeter, was carried off when she was playing and gathering flowers, and that the flower by which she was deceived into being carried off were not violets, but the narcissus." (Pausanias, *Description of Greece*, 9.31.9. trans. W.H.S. Jones)

To punish him, the goddess Νέμεσις, Nemesis, caused Narcissus to fall in love with his own reflection in a pool of water.[22] And so he fell in love with himself and he wasted away unto death, never being able to leave the image of his own reflection.[23]

We have become so accustomed to the common use and misuse of the Freudian term *narcissism* that we are likely to miss a valuable point of the myth of Narcissus. The Jungian analyst Edward Edinger brilliantly made this point in his book *Ego And Archetype*. Edinger pointed out that Narcissus

---

22   *Nemesis* was the goddess of Divine Retribution against mortals who succumbed to hubris, thus offending the gods. She was also called Ἀδράστεια, Adrastia. (*Ammianus Marcellinus* 14.11.25-26).

23   Ovid, *Metamorphoses*, Book III, 342-510.

represents the alienated ego that cannot love because it has not yet related to itself. It doesn't know itself.[24]

Remember the ancient Greek aphorism Γνῶθι Σεαυτόν, "Know Thyself"? It was one of the axioms inscribed on the pronaos of the Temple of Apollo at Delphi.[25] To know yourself does not mean to be familiar with your own image; we all know what we look like in the mirror — and it only gets worse every year I can promise you! We are not talking about being captivated or entranced by our own image. We are talking about actually coming to know *who we are* — to be in possession of our self.

If you are in love with the *reflection* of yourself, you

---

24   Edinger, *Ego and Archetype*, p. 161.
25   Pausanias, *Description of Greece*, 10.24.1.

are not yet in possession of yourself. Remember what *Liber LXV*, Chapter I, tells us in verse 7?

It says, "Be not contented with the image."

The result of this Narcissism is not that of a useless excess of self-love, but rather frustration and desire for a self-knowledge which does not exist. The unfulfilled yearning of Narcissus will only disappear with the experience of self-love.

Γνῶθι Σεαυτόν. "Know Thyself."

Edinger reminded us that fulfilled self-love is a prerequisite to being able to genuinely love anyone or anything.

To unite with the image in the water requires that we descend into the unconscious.[26] That is what Narcissus could not do. We have the basic idea in the vernacular of English when we say that someone "couldn't make the plunge." You have to dive in.

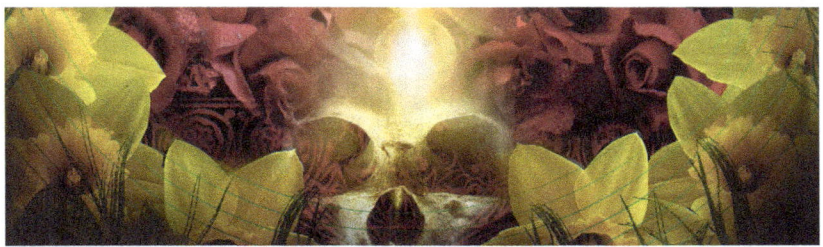

After he died, Narcissus the youth became the flower called Narcissus. The name Narcissus is from the

---

26   Edinger, *Ego and Archetype*, p.162.

Greek Ναρκάω, "to be stiff or dead."[27] The Narcissus is a death flower.[28] And here is something else that I find most interesting in this context: the etymology of the name Persephone is said to be φέρειν φόνον, which means "to bring or cause death."[29] Narcissus means to be dead, Persephone means to bring or cause death. I think I see a pattern here.

The Narcissus flower was sacred to Hades and opened the doors to the Underworld. Thus, when Persephone picked the Narcissus flower she unknowingly invoked the Lord of Hell.

The inescapable conclusion is that in order to enter the realm of the unconscious, one must experience Narcissus in the soul. Now, what does that mean?

---

27 *Narcissus* is connected with the word *Narcotic*, from the Greek Ναρκάω. (Skeat, *Concise Etymological Dictionary of the English Language*, p. 301a-b).

28 "It is *the flower of imminent death*, being associated, through its narcotic fragrance, with νάρκη —the pale beauty of the flower helping the thought. It is the *last* flower for which Persephone is stretching forth her hand when Pluto seizes her." (Jebb, *Sophocles, the Plays & Fragments*, Vol. 2, p. 115.) The Narcissus was anciently planted on new tombs. (Cf. Mackail, *Select Epigrams from the Greek Anthology*, Section XI "Death", No. 49, "Strewings for Graves", p. 283.)

29 Smith, *Dictionary of Greek and Roman Biography and Mythology*, Vol. 3, p. 204.

It means that you must first have a fulfilled expression of self-love — that is, self-knowledge — if you are to truly find love. And by love, I mean *Union*.

This self-love or self-knowledge involves going into the outermost places and confronting your fears, things that disgust you about yourself, and the weaknesses of your character.

"Go thou unto the outermost places and subdue all things. Subdue thy fear and thy disgust. Then — yield!"
***Liber LXV*, I:45-46**

This is the verse that immediately precedes our parable. This is the verse that the Angel uses to prepare us to receive the parable of Persephone.

You see, when you perform this difficult task, you begin to spiritually "grow up." You will have "*strayed among the corn*" so to speak, and will begin to grow a "*new birth.*"

You must be willing to leave your old life behind and seek a new one — still uncertain and unknown.

As I have often described it, you must abandon the **Death** which the world calls **Life**, and embrace the **Life** which the world calls **Death**.[30]

Now I do not want you to become confused with this symbolic language. You are *not* embracing death. You are embracing *life*. Remember that the etymology of Persephone's name meant to "cause or bring death"? Yes, but she grew a *new birth*. Your new birth will be a new flower in the fields, which the world will symbolically call Narcissus, the "death flower," because they cannot see the ineffable glory of the Path of the Adept, and its nameless goal. As it is written in *Liber Porta Lucis* verse 15:

"Even as a man ascending a steep mountain is lost to sight of his friends in the valley, so must the adept seem. They shall say: He is lost in the clouds. But he shall rejoice in the sunlight above them, and come to the eternal snows."

---

30   Cf. Gunther, *The Angel and The Abyss*, Chapter 1, "The Self Slain".

If you do that — begin to ascend the mountain — from that moment on, if you persist in the Path, you will be dead to the world, and the world with its former sense of values will be dead to you. The things of the world will not mean the same thing to you anymore. They will never have the same meaning for you *ever again*. Then, and only then, will you be ready to yield to the Holy Guardian Angel, and the little new plant will blossom into a beautiful flower. This is that which is written in *Liber VII*, Chapter 3, verses 56-57:

"Thou shalt crush me in the wine-press of Thy love.
My blood shall stain Thy fiery feet with litanies of Love in Anguish.
There shall be a new flower in the fields, a new vintage in the vineyards."

The new flower in the fields, the new vintage in the vineyards, is the Candidate, the "newly planted" one grown up — the Neophyte readied for the central Initiation. In the symbolism of the Neophyte Initiation Ritual of A∴A∴ the Candidate is the dead man *Asar*, Osiris the Lord of Death.

Transformed with self-knowledge, *Asar* becomes *Asar un Nefer*, Myself made Perfect.³¹

In the text of our Parable, Persephone picked the death plant. She experienced the Narcissus in her soul. She changed and grew a "new birth." So then what happened?

48. Even instantly rode Hades heavily upon her, and ravished her away.

The god of Hell came roaring out of the bowels of the earth and snatched her out of her sweet little former life, and forcibly carried her off into the depths of the Underworld. Note how the text of Verse 48 describes the appearance of Hades — "Even *instantly*" he rode heavily upon her.

---

31 In *Liber Samekh*, in Point I, Section A, no. 5, Crowley wrote, "Thou art ASAR-UN-NEFER ("Myself made Perfect".) The source document for *Liber Samekh* was a papyrus in the British Museum (Greek papyrus XLVI), published in 1852 e.v. under the name *Fragment of a Graeco-Egyptian Work Upon Magic*, translated by Charles Wycliffe Goodwin. In 1928 e.v. it was included in Karl Preisendanz' publication, *Papyri Graecae Magicae*, Vol. 1, pp. 184-186. An English translation of the PGM was published in in 1986 e.v. as *The Greek Magical Papyri In Translation*, by Hans Dieter Betz. Lines 96-172 of the papyrus fragment comprise the section that has come to be known as "The Bornless Ritual". Lines 101-102 read, Σὺ εἶ Ὀσορόννωφρις, ὅν οὐδεὶς εἶδε πώποτε, "Thou art *Osoronnophris* whom none hath ever seen". The name Ὀσορόννωφρις is a Greek corruption of the Egyptian 𓊨𓀭𓃹𓈖𓄤, *wsir-wn-nfr*, "Osiris the beautiful", or *Asar-un-nefer*. Crowley changed the corrupt Οσορόννωφρις to *Asar-un-nefer* for *Liber Samekh*, adding his magical interpretation, "Myself made Perfect".

So first, who does Hades signify? Does anyone here know the answer to that question? Yes, that's right. Hades signifies the Holy Guardian Angel.

figure 14

Those of you who read my first book, *Initiation in the Aeon of the Child*, may recall that in Chapter 8, titled "Wormwood," I quoted *The Vision & The Voice* from the 22nd Aethyr, where the Sevenfold Arrangement of *Hoor* is revealed, beginning with the revelation of the Three Aspects, which correspond to *Extraversion, Introversion* and *Centroversion*.[32]

Extraversion carries certain characteristics of the Aeon of the Father, the Aeon of Osiris. Introversion represents certain characteristics of the Aeon of the Mother, the Aeon of Isis. Centroversion of course is signified by the Aeon of the Child, the Aeon of Horus. Here is what is written in *The Vision & The Voice*:

"My arms were out in the form of a cross, and that Cross was extended, blazing with light into infinity. I myself am the minutest point in it. This is the *birth of form*."

---

32   See Gunther, *Initiation in the Aeon of the Child*, Chapter 8.

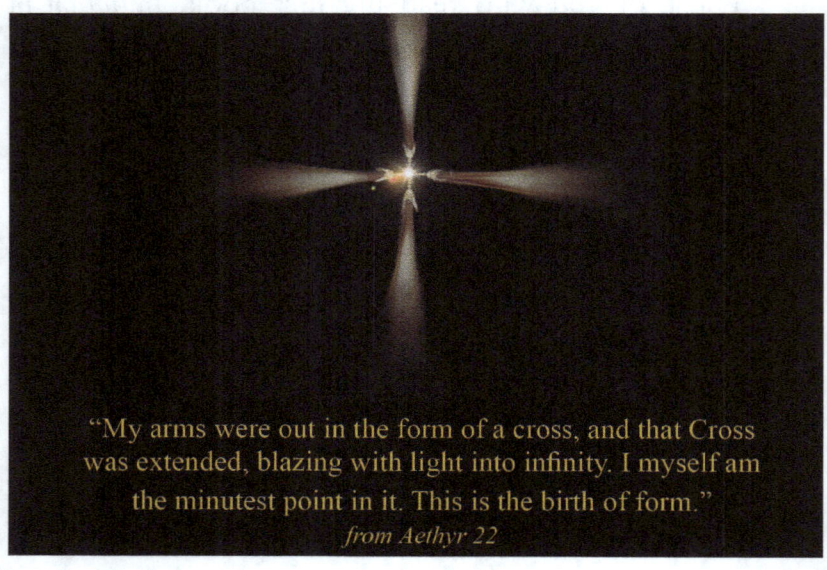

"My arms were out in the form of a cross, and that Cross was extended, blazing with light into infinity. I myself am the minutest point in it. This is the birth of form."
from Aethyr 22

The birth of form is the conception of the Self in extension — that is *Extraversion*.

"I am encircled by an immense sphere of many-coloured bands; it seems it is the sphere of the Sephiroth projected in the three dimensions. This is the birth of death."

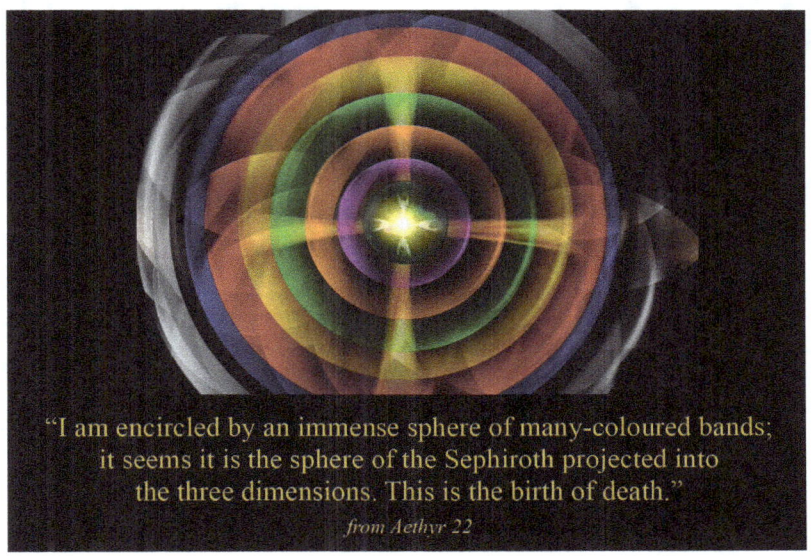

"I am encircled by an immense sphere of many-coloured bands; it seems it is the sphere of the Sephiroth projected into the three dimensions. This is the birth of death."
from Aethyr 22

The birth of *death* is the conception of the Self extended into the negative circle or sphere of Nuit — that is *Introversion*. You see? It's not scary at all!

This death is a death which should be *Infinite*, as *The Vision & The Voice* tells us. The death of the external world leads us to The Inward Journey.

And lastly, we see the Third and final aspect:

"Now in the centre within me is a glowing sun. That is the *birth of hell.*"

"Now in the centre within me is a glowing sun. That is the *birth of hell.*"
from Aethyr 22

This is referred to *Centroversion* — the perception of one's innermost Nature. It is particularly referred to the Aeon of the Child.

Look at this verse carefully: "Now in the centre within me is a glowing sun."

That is an image of *Tiphereth*, the Sixth Sephira on the Tree of Life to which we attribute the Sun — the "glowing sun" — the centre of humankind, the heart. It is the Sephira that corresponds to the Knowledge and Conversation of the Holy Guardian Angel. Remember the title of the book from which this Parable comes? *The Book of the Heart Girt with a Serpent.*

This is the birth of hell.
Apep deifieth Asar.[33]
What does *Liber Tzaddi* tell us?

"I have hidden myself beneath a mask: I am a black and terrible God.
With courage conquering fear shall ye approach me: ye shall lay down your heads upon mine altar, expecting the sweep of the sword.
But the first kiss of love shall be radiant on your lips;
and all my darkness and terror shall turn to light and joy."
Liber Tzaddi, 15-17

Those of you who will dare to "stray" among the corn, to grow a "new birth" — the Narcissus — you have the promise of the Lord of the Aeon in *Liber Tzaddi*, verses 27-30:

"O my children, ye are more beautiful than the flowers: ye must not fade in your season.
I love you; I would sprinkle you with the divine dew of immortality.
This immortality is no vain hope beyond the grave: I offer you the certain consciousness of bliss.
I offer it at once, on earth; before an hour hath struck upon

---

33   *Liber Stellæ Rubeæ*, 1.

the bell, ye shall be with Me in the Abodes that are beyond Decay"

At once. Even *instantly*. Before an hour hath struck upon the bell.
Look at this verse closely. Look at the last sentence. Do you see the words that are written in the Upper Case in mid-sentence?

Those words are: Me, Abodes, and Decay. M.A.D.
The letters M.A.D. spell the Enochian word = ℰ𐌙𐌎 *MADA*, which means "GOD"
Do you see ?
Before an hour hath struck upon the bell, *ye shall be with* God.

figure 6

The death flower, the Narcissus, will then be transformed into the *Chrysanthemum* — the Golden Flower. Ye shall be a new flower in the fields.

"O my children, ye are more beautiful than the flowers: ye must not fade in your season."

Amen.

LECTURE SERIES VOL. 1

PARABLES OF THELEMA
Part II

THE PARABLE OF THE PALE IMAGE

Liber LXV, Chapter 2, verses 7-16

Title Page Art: "Imago Aurea Asi in Navi Vitae," Annette Eustace Gray

τὰ ὄντα καὶ τὰ ἐσόμενα καὶ τὰ γεγονότα
ἐγώ εἰμι·
τὸν ἐμὸν χιτῶνα οὐδεὶς ἀπεκάλυψεν·
ὃν ἐγὼ καρπὸν ἔτεκον, ἥλιος ἐγένετο.

ΠΡΟΚΛΟΥ ΔΙΑΔΟΧΟΥ
ΕΙΣ ΤΟΝ ΤΙΜΑΙΟΝ ΠΛΑΤΩΝΟΣ
ΒΙΒΛΙΟΝ ΠΡΩΤΟΝ

List of Illustrations

p. 60	'River of blood,' *Annette Eustace Gray*.
p. 68	'Hadjar Silsilis, or the Rock of the Chain,' *The Holy Land, Syria, Idumea, Arabia, Egypt & Nubia, Vol. 5, Plate 180. (1856 e.v.)*
p. 69	'General View of the Ruins of Luxor from the Nile,' *The Holy Land, Syria, Idumea, Arabia, Egypt & Nubia, Vol. 4, Plate 141. (1856 e.v.)*
p. 70	Thomas Cole (ca. 1845 e.v.), *Macbeth Gallery Records, 1947-1948, Archives of American Art, Smithsonian Institution.*
p. 72	'The Voyage of Life – Childhood,' *Thomas Cole (1842 e.v.)*
p. 73	'The Voyage of Life – Childhood (detail),' *Thomas Cole (1842 e.v.)*
p. 75	'The Voyage of Life – Youth,' *Thomas Cole (1842 e.v.)*
p. 76	'The Voyage of Life – Manhood,' *Thomas Cole (1842 e.v.)*
p. 77	'The Voyage of Life – Old Age,' *Thomas Cole (1842 e.v.)*
p. 78	'The Voyage of Life - Old Age (detail),' *Thomas Cole (1842 e.v.)*

p. 79	'The Voyage of Life, four paintings,' *Thomas Cole (1842 e.v.)*
p. 81	'Gulf Stream,' *Winslow Homer (1899-1906 e.v.)*
p. 83	'Shades of Purple,' *Annette Eustace Gray.*
p. 86	'Imago Aurea Asi in Navi Vitae,' *Annette Eustace Gray.*
p. 89	'Osiris,' *The Egyptian Book of the Dead. The Papyrus of Ani, Plate 30b. (1894 e.v.)*
p. 90	'The Powers of the Sphinx,' *Ian Mercer.*
p. 92	'The Tzelim,' *Ian Mercer.*
p. 98	'She turned to blackness before me,' *Annette Eustace Gray & J. Daniel Gunther.*
p. 100	'Essence of the goddess,' *Annette Eustace Gray.*
p. 103	'Nigredo,' *Philosophia Reformata (1622 e.v.)*
p. 108	'Hadit,' *Jasenka Avram.*
p. 109	'The Saitic Isis,' *John Augustus Knapp (1928 e.v.)*

PARABLE OF THE PALE IMAGE

Do what thou wilt shall be the whole of the Law.

Today, I would like to discuss the Parable which is found in *Liber LXV*, Chapter 2, verses 7-16. I call it, "The Parable of the Pale Image."

7. Moreover I beheld a vision of a river. There was a little boat thereon; and in it under purple sails was a golden woman, an image of Asi wrought in finest gold. Also the river was of blood, and the boat of shining steel. Then I loved her; and, loosing my girdle, cast myself into the stream.
8. I gathered myself into the little boat, and for many days and nights did I love her, burning beautiful incense before her.
9. Yea! I gave her of the flower of my youth.
10. But she stirred not; only by my kisses I defiled her so that she turned to blackness before me.
11. Yet I worshipped her, and gave her of the flower of my youth.
12. Also it came to pass, that thereby she sickened, and corrupted before me. Almost I cast myself into the stream.
13. Then at the end appointed her body was whiter than the

milk of the stars, and her lips red and warm as the sunset, and her life of a white heat like the heat of the midmost sun.

14. Then rose she up from the abyss of Ages of Sleep, and her body embraced me. Altogether I melted into her beauty and was glad.
15. The river also became the river of Amrit, and the little boat was the chariot of the flesh, and the sails thereof the blood of the heart that beareth me, that beareth me.
16. O serpent woman of the stars! I, even I, have fashioned Thee from a pale image of fine gold.

The Parable

Since there are ten verses that comprise this parable, let's break it down into more convenient sections, beginning with Verse 7. Now, I will refer to the one narrating these Verses as "the Scribe," in this case meaning *Frater Perdurabo* or *Aleister Crowley*.

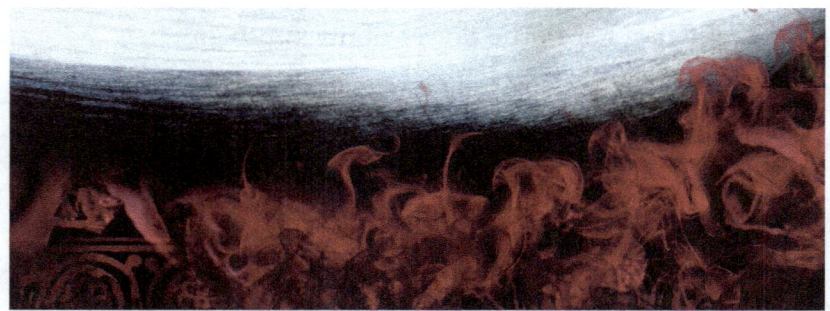

7. Moreover I beheld a vision of a river. There was a little boat thereon; and in it under purple sails was a golden woman, an image of Asi wrought in finest gold. Also the river was of blood, and the boat of shining steel. Then I loved her; and, loosing my girdle, cast myself into the stream.

The Scribe begins with a vision of a river. In Crowley's commentary to this verse, he said, "Verses 7-16: The river is the stream of thought. The boat is the consciousness." With all due respect, I believe that his interpretation here is entirely incorrect. He wasn't paying close enough attention to the wording of the Holy Book. In Verse 15, it states explicitly that the boat is the "chariot of flesh." It represents human incarnation. It is the *river* that is the stream of *consciousness*, not the boat.

In this context, I include the components of the *personal unconscious* as well, since its contents are derived from the conscious stream.[1]

At this point, we are only concerned with the elements of our *personal consciousness* and *personal unconscious*.

---

[1] "The contents of the personal unconscious...constitute the personal and private side of psychic life." (Jung, *Archetypes of the Collective Unconscious*, p. 4.)

Consciousness & Unconsciousness

The unconscious has two distinct aspects: the *personal unconscious* and the *collective unconscious*. The components of one's personal unconscious were once conscious. They may have been simply forgotten, or repressed — or stored away to make room for more current conscious activity.² In many circumstances, the components of the personal unconscious can be retrieved. They are still there, but they lie in the murky area beyond the fringes of our consciousness.

Qabalistically, we say that personal consciousness formulates in the *Hexad of the Intellect*,³ which is centered in the Sephira תפארת, *Tiphereth*, in what we call the רוח, *Ruach*.⁴

In this relationship, we must exclude our instincts, or what we call the נפש, *Nephesh*, or "animal soul," which are attributed to מלכות, *Malkuth*, the tenth and pendant Sephira beyond this Hexad on the Tree of Life. The instincts

---

2   "...the personal unconscious is made up essentially of components which have at one time been conscious but which have disappeared from consciousness through having been forgotten or repressed..." (*Ibid.*, p. 42.)

3   The Hexad of the Intellect is comprised of the aggregate of six Sephiroth: חסד *Chesed*, גבורה *Geburah*, תפארת *Tiphereth*, נצח *Netzach*, הוד *Hod* and יסוד *Yesod*. We say that consciousness *formulates* there, not necessarily *originating* there.

4   See the Frontispiece of this book, p. 12.

are common to animals as well as humans, operating without conscious intent or direction. In the words of Carl Jung: "instincts are impersonal, universally distributed, hereditary factors of a dynamic or motivating character, which very often fail...to reach consciousness... Moreover, the instincts are not vague and indefinite by nature, but are specifically formed motive forces which, long before there is any consciousness, and in spite of any degree of consciousness later on, pursue their inherent goals."[5]

The collective unconscious is dissimilar from the personal unconscious in that its contents are primordial components, which are called *archetypes*, which have *never* been conscious.[6]

We must distinguish the *primordial* archetypes that anciently became conscious and have been converted into conscious formulae, typically expressed through the centuries in religious or esoteric teachings. Technically, these components are no longer archetypes for they have been contaminated with consciousness and are now available for

---

5   Jung, *op.cit.* p. 43.

6   "The collective unconscious is a part of the psyche which can be negatively distinguished from a personal unconscious by the fact that it does not, like the latter, owe its existence to personal experience and consequently is not a personal acquisition...the contents of the collective unconscious have never been in consciousness, and therefore have never been individually acquired, but owe their existence exclusively to heredity...the content of the collective unconscious is made up essentially of *archetypes*." *(loc.cit.)*

conscious elaboration. Although these elaborations appear in consciousness, they are not intellectual manipulations and interpretations. They occurred naturally, adapted by the cultures in which they appeared, taking on unique characteristics while retaining elements of the original motif. The term "archetypes" only applies while they are formless factors prior to interaction with consciousness.

The River of Life

Returning now to Verse 7 of Liber LXV, we should note that the nature of a river is quite apt for a symbol of consciousness. The flowing surface of the water is like our active consciousness, ever-moving, ever-changing, but visible. In the sense of consciousness, it is that which is perceivable. Those things which lie in the depths of that river are concealed, that is, these components are the personal unconscious. They may arise on their own, or may be brought to the surface by conscious effort; they can also remain unconscious. We are justified in calling it the "river of Life" because as we see, it is described as a "river of blood."

In the Old Testament book of *Deuteronomy*, Moses said, הדם הוא הנפש, "the blood is the life," a phrase appreciated and quoted by Bram Stoker in his novel *Dracula*.[7] The Hebrews were allowed to eat the flesh of

---

7   Stoker, *Dracula* (1897), p. 142, "Dr. Seward's Diary."

animals, but were forbidden to consume the blood, for the life was therein:

רק חזק לבלתי אכל הדם כי הדם הוא הנפש
ולא־תאכל הנפש עם־הבשר:

"*Only, be sure not to eat the blood, for the blood is the life, and thou shalt not eat the life with the flesh.*" [8]

Lest you think that disease prevention was the reason they were forbidden to eat blood, you must not forget that the blood of those animals, as well as their burned flesh, was a sacrifice *required* by Yahweh.

ועשית עלתיך הבשר והדם על־מזבח יהוה אלהיך
ודם־זבחיך ישפך על־מזבח יהוה אלהיך

"*And thou shalt offer thy burnt offerings, the flesh and the blood, on the altar of Yahweh thy God; and the blood of thy sacrifices shall be poured out upon the altar of Yahweh thy God.*" [9]

Although the consumption of blood was forbidden to the Hebrews, it was poured out upon the altar to be symbolically consumed by *Yahweh himself*. To what end? It was to atone for the sins of his Chosen People.

---

8   *Deuteronomy* 12:23.

9   *Deuteronomy* 12:27.

ואיש איש מבית ישראל ומן־הגר הגר בתוכם אשר יאכל כל־דם ונתתי פני בנפש האכלת את־הדם והכרתי אתה מקרב עמה: כי נפש הבשר בדם הוא ואני נתתיו לכם על־המזבח לכפר על־נפשתיכם כי־הדם הוא בנפש יכפר:

> *"And any man of the house of Israel, or of the foreigners sojourning in thy midst, who consumes any blood, I will set my face against that person who consumes blood, and will cut him off from the midst of his people. For the life of the flesh is in the blood and I have given it to thee upon the altar to atone for thy souls; for it is the blood that atones for the soul."* [10]

This ritual was based on the pernicious Old Aeonic doctrine that without the shedding of blood there is no salvation.

This is reiterated in the New Testament, in the book of *Hebrews*, a text written for Jews, with the purpose of demonstrating that the blood sacrifice of Jesus satisfied the thirst of Yahweh in order to atone for the sins of all humankind.

---

10   *Leviticus* 17:10-11.

καὶ σχεδὸν ἐν αἵματι πάντα καθαρίζεται
κατα τὸν νόμον, καὶ χωρὶς αἱματεκχθσίας οὐ
γίνεται ἄφεσις

"And almost all things are purified with blood according to the Law, and apart from the shedding of blood there is no forgiveness." [11]

For those who accept the Law of Thelema, the blood is still the life – our free lives — no longer chained in bondage at the superstitious whim of any slave god. We are free to give our life blood — the essence of our life — as we Will.

The "river of blood." This is the river of our lives. The life is in the blood.[12]

The river of blood is the river of consciousness.

---

11   *Epistle to the Hebrews* 9:22.

12   See Crowley, *Book IV, Part III, Chapter XII*, "Of the Bloody Sacrifice, and of Matters Cognate."

Now, on this river, the Scribe beholds a little boat. Note that he calls it a "little boat." Think of a small sailboat. It gives us a sense of intimacy — we are not talking about a boat large enough for a number of people — a small boat.

There is no one in the boat yet. But we know that the Scribe intends to symbolize each of us — *each of us*, eventually in our own boat on this river of consciousness.

You know, the symbol of a boat signifying an individual's life has its roots in the distant past. In ancient Egypt, one's life was imagined as a journey down the holy river. The Nile was literally the life blood of Egypt.[13]

---

13   The Greek Historian Herodotus wrote: δῆλα γὰρ δὴ καὶ μὴ προακούσαντι ἰδόντι δέ, ὅστις γε σύνεσιν ἔχει, ὅτι Αἴγυπτος, ἐς τὴν Ἕλληνες ναυτίλλονται, ἐστὶ Αἰγυπτίοισι ἐπίκτητός τε γῆ καὶ δῶρον τοῦ ποταμοῦ...

The Egyptians considered everything on earth to be a reflection of that which was in the sky. The Nile was the reflection of the Milky Way in their eyes. A human lifetime was considered to be a journey down the starry river of life.

One of the ancient Egyptian euphemisms for dying was ![glyph], *mni,* to moor the boat." To die was to bring the boat of life to harbor (![glyph], *mniwt.*)[14]

Spell 18 from the *Egyptian Book of the Dead* ends with

"For if even a man has not heard it before, if he has sense he can readily see that Egypt, to which the Greeks sail, is land deposited for the Egyptians, a gift of the river." (Herodotus 2.5.1. Greek text in Stein, *Herodotos*, Vol. 2, p. 9). This quote has been commonly paraphrased as "Egypt is the gift of the Nile."

14   CDME, *pp.* 107-108.

the following passage which illustrates this usage:

"If a man recites this Spell when pure, it assures going out in the day after his mooring (i.e. his death.)" [15]

Speaking of the "river of life," I am also remined of a

---

15   *ḏd s r pn wꜥb prt pw m hrw m-ḫt mni=f* Papyrus of Nu, BM 10477, 18,4 (sheet 4).

series of four paintings by the American artist Thomas Cole which he painted in 1842 e.v. Thomas Cole is considered the founder of the Hudson River School, an art movement that emphasized realistic portrayals of nature, strongly infused with Romanticism.[16]

These paintings were collectively called "*The Voyage of Life*,"[17] and were given sub-titles that signify the four stages of human life: *Childhood, Youth, Manhood,* and *Old Age*. They provide us one way of looking at this river.

---

16   A overly sentimental biography of Thomas Cole was written in 1853 by Louis L. Noble, a Christian clergyman, entitled *The Course of Empire, Voyage of Life, and other pictures of Thomas Cole*. It was reprinted in 1964 by Harvard University Press as *The Life and Works of Thomas Cole*, with an introduction by Elliot S. Vesell.

17   Cole was originally commissioned in 1839 e.v. by Samuel Ward, Sr. to produce this series of paintings. Ward died unexpectedly a few months later before the works were completed in 1840. The heirs of Samuel Ward refused to allow the works being placed on public display. Cole painted them again, with notable improvements over the originals, and these were publicly displayed for the first time. The original paintings are now held in the *Munson-Williams-Proctor Arts Institute* in Utica, New York. The second set is in the *National Gallery of Art* in Washington D.C.

The first painting in the series is called "Childhood."

This composition introduced the key elements in the entire series: the small boat, the river, the Holy Guardian Angel, the voyager, and a panoramic landscape.

The boat has exited a dark cave that is symbolic of the womb. It is just setting out on life's journey on the river of life. The river ahead is narrow and calm and the sky is clear and blue in the distance. Flowers bloom among the lush vegetation along the river bank. The entire scene is idyllic, representing the innocence of childhood.

If we examine a close-up of the boat, we see clearly that the passenger is but a baby, surrounded by flowers in fresh bloom; the child appears to be bouncing with delight. Note that the Angel holds the tiller of the boat directing its course with the right hand; the left hand is placed protectively over the child.

At the bow of the boat, the figurehead is comprised of Angelic figures. The symbolism of the figurehead on ships date back thousands of years. Such figures of deities were a type of talisman intended to protect the vessel and its sailors. The nautical figurehead became a prominent feature on sailing vessels between the 16th and 19th centuries as a way to designate the name of the vessel for illiterate sailors, or to demonstrate the wealth and power of the owners.[18] One

---

[18] Thomov, *Four Scandinavian Ship Graffiti from Hagia Sophia. In Byzantine and Modern Greek Studies*, Vol. 38, No. 2, pp. 168-184. Morrison, *Greek and Roman Oared Warships* 399-30 B.C., p. 209.

of the earliest precursors to the nautical figurehead was the placement of a statue in the bow of a boat. The ancient Egyptians depicted the goddess Isis in the bow of a barque, a figure which evolved in Hellenistic times as the prominent figure of *Isis Pelagia*, "Isis of the Seas," adorning the bows of ships.[19] The parallel to the imagery of this Parable is striking.

In the painting "Childhood" by Thomas Cole, the Angelic figureheads on the little boat are intended to serve as a reminder of the divine nature that created and guides the vessel of life. They embody the spirit of this boat. Yet note that the standing Angel in the figurehead leans precipitously forward, holding an *hourglass* aloft with both hands.

The hourglass signifies Time. The Angel seems to eagerly lean forward, holding the hourglass as if it were a lamp to light the darkness. Yet, this is not the message of this image.

The Arrow of Time only goes forward, never backward. This figure reminds us that at the very beginning of this Voyage of Life, the sands of time have already begun to pass through the hourglass, and one day they will run out.

The second painting in the series by Thomas Cole is called "Youth."

---

19   See Bricault, *Isis Pelagia: Images, Names and Cults of a Goddess of the Seas, passim*.

We now see the young man grasp the tiller of the boat for himself. The Angel has disembarked the vessel and is standing on the shore waving farewell as the youth sets out on his journey.

The river is calm and serene. If we look closely, we can see the confidence and energy of the youth. He leans forward in a posture that emulates the Angelic figurehead at the bow of the boat, as if eagerly urging the boat down stream. So it is with youth: many of us rushed in where Angels fear to tread.

In the distance, we can see a grand, ghostly Palace in the clouds, which represents the young man's dreams and aspirations. Behind the well-formulated Palace in the foreground, there are the faint images of other turrets or minarets disappearing into the distance. This tells us that his dreams and hopes are endless at this stage in his life. The horizon seems to go on forever.

With the third painting, Cole depicted Manhood.

Our young man is now grown. The boat has been damaged by the ravages of time and experience.

The river is now depicted with whitewater rapids; a dangerous waterfall looms just ahead. Even in the landscape, we see how Cole has emphasized danger and foreboding. There are broken and gnarled trees, craggy rocks in the place of green grass, a dark and gloomy sky of storm clouds and pouring rain.

The tiller is gone; the man has no means to steer the vessel. Thus, no longer in control of his boat, the man prays to God for salvation. His Angel, which he cannot see, still watches over him.

We can see that Angel behind and above him in a gleaming aureole among the brooding storm clouds. We further note that the Angelic figurehead is still intact, still serving as the masthead on the boat of the man's journey as it approaches the perilous rapids ahead.

The final painting is named "Old Age."

We see that the river of life is once again quiet and calm. The time of danger has passed, and with it, the entire landscape, except for a few dim rocks of the shoreline.

There are no more daydream Castles in the sky. There is no endless horizon that lies ahead; the man is coming to the end of his journey.

The boat in which he sits bears the scars of his lifetime. It is beaten and battered, but still afloat.

    He tentatively extends both arms in the direction of the Angel above him. In the gesture of open arms we can sense his readiness to disembark his boat.

    When we examine this painting in detail, we see the further damage that time has inflicted upon his vessel: the figurehead of the Angel that bore the hourglass has broken off. The man has run out of time.

    All that remains visibly of the Angelic figures that had adorned the bow of the boat is a single golden Angel. Its back toward us, but its head turned, as it were, toward the gleaming light of the heavens to which the Angel gestures with one hand, while gently reaching out to the man with the other, urging him to follow.

    And in that gleaming light, Angels are descending from heaven. The Holy Guardian Angel of the old man leads the way.

Thomas Cole himself described this scene: "The chains of corporeal existence are falling away; and already the mind has glimpses of Immortal Life."[20]

Now, there is no question that Cole intended these paintings as allegories of his Christian faith. He painted these in 1842 e.v., at a time when the United States had just experienced a great Protestant movement called "The Second Great Awakening," which railed against the evils of society and the need to prepare for the second advent of Jesus Christ.[21]

---

20   Noble, *The Life and Works of Thomas Cole, N. A.*, p. 289.

21   See Ahlstrom, *A Religious History of the American People* (2004) for a good overview of the evolution of Christian denominations in the United States, and Birdsall, *The Second Great Awakening and the New England Social Order* (1970) for an analysis of the movement and its beginnings in New England.

These paintings were very popular, of course; they are extravagantly sentimental, with a "sugar won't melt in your mouth" romanticized religiosity. Yet within them, we can see manifestations of a number of Archetypal motifs that not only pervade the Christianity of Thomas Cole, but our system as well.

Other painters, more influenced by experience than romanticism, expressed similar motifs with just a bit more grit.

One such example is the great American artist Winslow Homer, who in 1899 e.v., produced a painting which he named "Gulf Stream." When it was shown in 1900-1901 e.v., the critic Sadakichi Hartmann called it "one of the greatest pictures ever painted in America." Not all critics were as charitable.[22]

Homer's bleak composition features a black man adrift on a battered sailboat; the mast has been torn away, leaving a useless sail draped over the gunwale. The hapless sailor lies near a few stalks of sugar cane on which he has subsisted.

---

22   Spassky, *American paintings in the Metropolitan Museum of Art*. Vol. II, pp. 483-489.

Now he gazes into the distance, his boat encircled by hungry sharks, and seemingly unaware of the threatening water spout approaching. He is likewise oblivious to the schooner in the misty distance that might offer hope of rescue.

He is clearly resigned to his fate.

There seems little doubt that Homer's intention was to create a composition that reflected the helpless plight of man confronted with his inevitable demise.

He began this painting the year that his own father died.[23]

---

23   Homer began this work in 1898 e.v. and completed it in 1899 e.v. (Ibid. p. 482) His father died in 1898 e.v. (Downes, *The Life and Works of Winslow Homer*, p. 115). Some recent critics have misinterpreted some of Homer's paintings as evidence of prejudicial racial disparity without consideration of the fact that his models were depicted as they appeared

Homer's painting is quite removed from the romantic style of Thomas Cole's works. The thing they share in common is the boat as an emblem of life's journey. Like all earthly journeys, there is a beginning and there is an end.

Now, let us return to our parable.

The Pale Image of Fine Gold

7.   **Moreover I beheld a vision of a river. There was a little boat thereon; and in it under purple sails was a golden woman, an image of Asi wrought in finest gold. Also the river was of blood, and the boat of shining steel. Then I loved her; and, loosing my girdle, cast myself into the stream.**

In this Vision, our little sailboat has *purple sails*. Let's not skip past this small but very important detail. Purple was traditionally considered the Royal or Episcopal color. It was the color worn by Roman Magistrates, and later by Roman Catholic Bishops. Hence, it is now associated with Royalty or Piety.[24] It is formed from the combination of Red and Blue.

---

in situ, without any intent of social commentary. In his time, Homer was criticized by some for using black people for his subjects, which many white elititists of that time considered an inferior subject. He was an artist, not a social activist. Homer was inspired by the people in his world, regardless of skin color or social status.

24   Heller, *Psychologie de la Couleur, Effets et Symboliques*, p. 162.

For those of you who don't paint, let me pass on a few details about this color that you may find helpful. Purple occupies the space on the color wheel between Crimson and Violet, but closer to red.

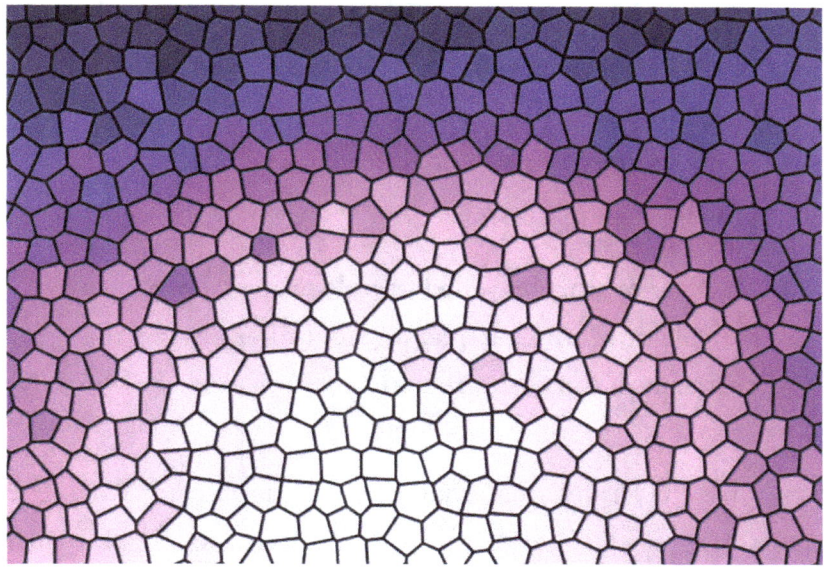

The color Violet itself is closer to blue, and is usually less intense and bright as Purple, which is a combination of Red and Blue — but with more Red. Here is a really important point: Purple and Violet are *not* the same. Violet is one of the colors in the *Visible Spectrum*. It has its own wavelength of light. Purple does not. Purple is a color that we can make by mixing pigments or dyes. But it does not occur in the Universal Spectrum of Light Waves.[25]

---

25   Violet has a wavelength of 380-450 nanometers, the lowest number in the visible spectrum of light, the lowest visible to the human

So, what does this tell us? The sails are not violet — they are *purple*. It is a color that was deliberately made. The Sails represent a device of human construction, devised for a single purpose, and given a deliberate color.

That's why Crowley said purple signified "heavenly or starry existence manifested through the principle of blood or animal life."[26] In his commentary to Liber LXV, he described the purple sails of the boat as the "passions that direct its course."

> "...Pale or purple, veiled or voluptuous, I who am all pleasure and purple, and drunkenness of the innermost sense, desire you."
>
> *Liber AL*, I:61

We may note here that in the Chapter of *Nuit*, the first Chapter of *The Book of the Law*, "pale" is aligned with "veiled," in contrast to "purple" which is aligned with "voluptuous." Nuit then describes herself as "all pleasure and purple." This is a pretty good example of Crowley's definition of "heavenly or starry existence manifested through the principle of blood or animal life."

The sails indicate the element of air, or breath. Well, that is what makes the boat of our life move isn't it? If we're not breathing, I would say it won't be long before we are

---

eye. Cf. Gilbert & Haeberli, *Physics in the Arts*, pp. 82-83 and p. 112.

26   Crowley, *Liber 777*, note to Column XV, 3.

mooring that boat.

The ancient Egyptian word for "breath" or "wind" or "air", was 🪶, *ṯ3w*.[27] The first hieroglyph in this word represents the sails of a boat. In the case of our parable, the purple sails are a bit more than our passion to direct the course of the boat — that is, to perform the Great Work — they indicate the means to capture *Divine Inspiration*.

The word "Inspire" means literally, "to breathe into." It's a combination of "In" and "Spirit."[28] The Latin word *Spiritus* means "breathing."[29] Greek πνεῦμα means "breath."[30] The Hebrew parallel is the word רוּחַ, *Ruach*, which means simply, "breath."[31] The concept of Spirit has been historically connected with Air and Breath. Living. Breathing.

Here, in the Scribe's vision of the little boat, we see that it has been outfitted with Purple Sails to catch the Divine Breath to help move it down the River of Life.

And the boat? It is made of *shining steel*.

Now, here is a curious symbolism. Steel?

Why not wood, like the sailboats of old?

Steel is a *human-made substance*, that's why. We can

---

27   CDME, p. 303.

28   Skeat, p. 296.

29   OLD Vol. 2, p.1991a.

30   LSJ, p.1424a, 2.

31   Gesenius, p. 760a.

shape wood, form it to suit our pleasure, but we can't make it. Steel is an alloy of Carbon and Iron. It was produced thousands of years ago in bloomery furnaces. The process was refined during the 17th to the 19th Centuries.

The boat is of "shining steel" — polished, of human fabrication. Its sails are purple — dyed a specific color, also of human composition. So, once again, we know the boat is the boat of humankind on a spiritual journey down this long river, even though as yet, there is no one in the boat. It is still unmanned.

Beneath these sails in the little boat, there is something wonderful — a golden image, in finest gold, of 𓊃𓏏𓁥 , *3st, Asi* — that is, the goddess Isis.³²

Isis signifies the *Divine life in Nature*. But remember — and this is very important — in the context of this parable, even though she is made of Gold, she is merely a *lifeless image* of the real thing.

Now, beholding this vision of the golden Isis, the Scribe falls in love with her. He falls in love with the Ideal, Divine Image of Nature.

He loosens his girdle — meaning here, the belt that constrains his garments —the fetters of Reason that bind him — and he dives into the river of blood.³³

"Then I loved her; and, loosing my girdle, cast myself into the stream."

In other words, he tries to release the bonds of his *ego* and then plunge into the stream of pure consciousness — the river of blood.

He leaps in the stream and begins swimming toward the boat.

Why do I limit the symbol of the *girdle* to the processes of the רוח, *Ruach*, or Reasoning Faculty? Because he says

---

32   CDME, p.5.

33   The word *girdle* is derived from *gird*, "to enclose, bind round." (*Skeat*, p. 234b).

explicitly, "I loved her." Love is not a process of the Reason. It is of the נפש, *Nephesh*, the Emotions.

Love, not Reason, is what prompts him to loosen his girdle and plunge into the stream. I do not need to remind you that the Intellectual "girdle" of Aleister Crowley was a substantial retainer.

Further, it should be noted that it does not say he *removed* his girdle — he *loosened it*. Admittedly, at first blush, we have the impression that this meant he became naked. But the Holy Book doesn't say that.[34] However, loosening the girdle allows more freedom of movement. That is what I believe is meant here. Many times during our personal practices, we must loosen the grip of the Intellect *just enough* to *yield* to the experience.

We have another example in the Holy Books of this same terminology and symbolism. *Liber VII*, Chapter 7, Verses 1 and 2 offer a lovely symbolic description of the *Cakes of Light*;[35] Verse 3 follows with a description of one of the mystic results that these Cakes can initiate:

> **"These loosen the swathings of the corpse; these unbind the feet of Osiris, so that the flaming God**

---

[34] We must always pay close attention to the *exact* words used in our Sacred Texts lest we fall into errors of misunderstanding at best, or textual corruption at worst.

[35] See Crowley, *Book IV, Part III*, Chapter XX, "*Of the Eucharist; and of the Art of Alchemy*." See also *Liber AL* III:23.

may rage through the firmament with his fantastic spear."

The Egyptian god 𓊨𓁹, *wsir,* Osiris, the Lord of the dead, was the icon of death and resurrection for the Egyptians. He was normally depicted in the form of a mummy, bound from foot to neck in bandages: the "swathings of the corpse."

In the System of A∴A∴, the symbolism of Osiris is utilized to signify the beginning Aspirant to Initiation, bound by the torpor and inertia of the profane world. Every Candidate for Initiation is initially identified with Osiris

(Asar), struggling against the sleep of death, oblivious to the Higher Aspirations.[36]

The fetters that bind the Will of the Aspirant must be loosened in order for them to manifest the 5th Power of the Sphinx, IRE, "To Go", and release the Child within them, the flaming God Horus. Magically, in their ongoing private practices, the Cakes of Light can be an aid in that effort. In this example from Liber VII, the restraints are not removed, but "loosened" enough to unbind the feet to allow mobility.

---

36   See Gunther, *The Angel & The Abyss*, Chapter 1, *The Self-Slain*.

Likewise, in Verse 7 of Liber LXV, Chapter 2, the Scribe doesn't remove his garments, but "loosens" his girdle to allow mobility that he may swim. His newly-found love for the goddess overcomes intellectual circumspection enough to allow himself to leap from the bank and plunge into the stream that he might swim to reach her.

But he's made a mistake right here, and doesn't know it. What has he done?

He has become transfixed in one sense by the *Fatal Image of Nature*.

Now, he has not fallen in love with the profane world — which is how we most often see a candidate derailed by the Fatal Image of Nature. He has fallen in love with its *Ideal Image*. Here is a color version of a drawing I placed in my first book:

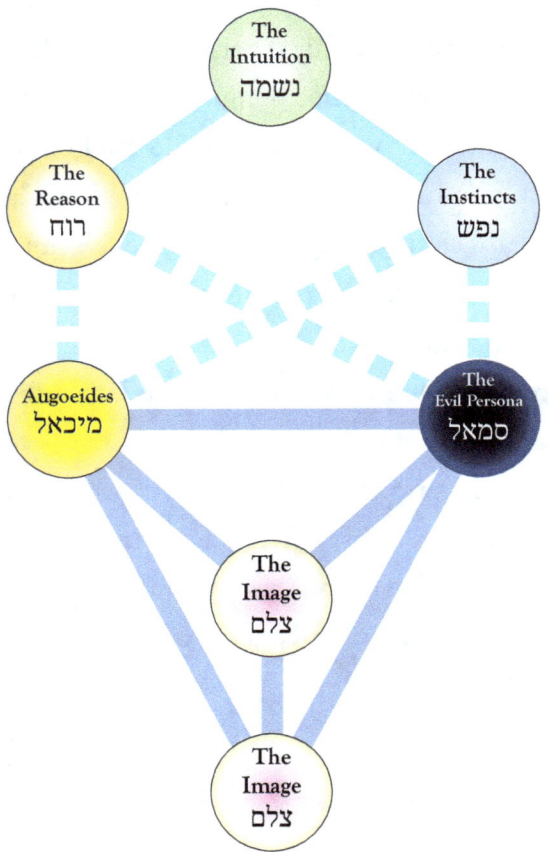

The צלם, *Tzelim*, or "Image" — This is a drawing based on the original designed by Éliphas Lévi and later utilized by S. L. Mathers.[37]

As you can see from this diagram, there are two Images. They exist in a house of mirrors. You can see the Image of

---

37   Lévi, *La clef des grands mystères* (1861), p. 389, and Mathers, *Kabbala Denudata, The Kabbalah Unveiled* (1887) plate facing page 37.

Augoeides[38] or the Holy Guardian Angel, or the Image of the *Evil Persona*, or the Image of the Image of either one.

I wrote in *Initiation in the Aeon of the Child* that both of these images must be ignored — whether it be the Image of the Holy One, or the Image of the Evil Persona.[39] We do not have the intellectual means to discriminate between them — they are both Phantoms of the real thing. That is one reason why we are admonished in *Liber LXV*, Chapter 1, Verse 7:

"Be not contented with the image."

Very simply, the image is not the real thing. On the Path of Initiation you must be very careful about this error.

I see people, all the time, captivated by an image of Nuit, or Ra-Hoor-Khuit, or The Beast, or Aleister Crowley the man, or whatever. They become enamored and blinded by the glamor of these things. Those who seek the Holy Guardian Angel can also fall into this ditch as well. That is why I wrote about *The Vision of the Holy Guardian Angel* in my first book — it is not a "Vision" at all.[40]

---

38   αὐγοειδής is a Greek word meaning, "of the nature of light" (*LSJ, p.* 274b.) See *The Angel & The Abyss*, pp. 311-314.

39   See Gunther, *Initiation in the Aeon of the Child*, Chapter 6, ע, *The Image of God*, pp.128-129. The Evil Persona is the negative aspects of the personality, which Jungian Psychology calls "The Shadow."

40   Gunther, *Initiation in the Aeon of the Child*, Chapter 6, p. 127

8. I gathered myself into the little boat, and for many days and nights did I love her, burning beautiful incense before her.
9. Yea! I gave her of the flower of my youth.

So our young aspirant takes the plunge into the River of Life, and swims toward the golden image with which he had fallen in love. When he reaches the boat, he pulls himself up and climbs in.

Then he begins a Ritual. For many days and nights he adores her and burns lovely incense before her image.

Look closely at verse 9: "Yea! I gave her of the flower of my youth."

What flower is that do you think? Does anyone have an idea?

It's the same flower that I discussed in the lecture of the *Parable of the New Birth*. It's the flower of the "new birth."[41]

The so-called "flower of our youth" is defined as that period in our life when we are young and at our best and most active. For an Initiate, that is the flower of your "new birth" — and it doesn't necessarily have anything to do with your age in years — it has to do with your age as a young Initiate.

You may have taken up the Great Work when you were 20 or 30 or 40 years old. Here, we are not talking about

---

41   See Gunther, *The Parable of the New Birth*, passim.

your profane life when you were that age. We're talking about your *Initiatic* life. It may have been when you were 20 years old. But not necessarily.

In my travels a few years ago, I met a lovely woman who was 77 years of age. In the twilight of her life, she had discovered Thelema. In her case, the flower of her youth — the flower of her "new birth" — was the Narcissus, the death flower. They were, for her, one and the same.

Not long after I met her, she was diagnosed with stage IV metastatic colon cancer. Her physicians estimated that she only had about a year to live.

As her conditioned worsened, she realized that she would not have much time left. She made a special request of her OTO Lodge, telling them that she wanted to hear me lecture one more time before the end came. Graciously, her Lodge granted her request, and at considerable expense, flew my wife Gwen and myself across the USA so that I could give two more lectures, just for her.

Although she was in great pain, she sat in the front row and hung on my every word as best she could. After the lectures were over, she came to me privately and asked for a special favor. When I asked her what I could do for her, she replied, "I want you to teach me how to die. Will you come to my home this evening?"

I was deeply humbled by her request, but naturally, I agreed to do so.

That evening at her home, we sat alone in her parlor,

and we spoke openly and candidly about the task of confronting impending death.

At the end of our conversation, she said, "I grieve only because I'm just getting started."

Holding her hand, I replied, "Yes, you were just getting started. But do not grieve. You are about to come to harbor and moor this tired, damaged boat. Then, after a moment of rest, you will take the flower of this life with you, and in a new, young vessel, set out once again upon the River of Life for this splendid journey."

She smiled through her tears and said emphatically, "Yes, I will."

Not long after that, she died.

The true flower of youth can bloom at any stage of our life. We are fortunate if it does so while our bodies are young and strong.

Now, our young aspirant in the boat confessed that he had spent the currency that is the flower of his youth on this Golden image of the goddess. He worshipped her. He adored her. He had burned incense in her name — for many days and nights.

10. But she stirred not; only by my kisses I defiled her so that she turned to blackness before me.
11. Yet I worshipped her, and gave her of the flower of my youth.

12. Also it came to pass, that thereby she sickened, and corrupted before me. Almost I cast myself into the stream.

As we might expect, the "image" did not stir; it did not move. It did not respond to any of his adorations.

In our imagination now, we can see the aspirant in the boat, kissing that statue again and again, until the Gold becomes soiled and marred with black stains.

Everyone close your eyes. I want you to form a clear image of that little boat with the purple sails — a statue of Isis beneath the sails.

Now, imagine yourself as that aspirant, burning incense before her, kissing the statue over and over again.

The river is calm and still. No breeze stirs the sails. Still, you continue to adore the statue and kiss it as if it were your lover.

Now, time passes. And you see that wherever you have kissed the statue it has begun to become soiled and black, obscuring the sheen of the Gold. The more you kiss it, the blacker it becomes. The image of the goddess sickens before your eyes.

Keep your eyes closed. Hold that image, but listen to my words now.

Gold will never react with Oxygen and so it cannot tarnish or rust. But it is a fact that human perspiration and saliva can leave a superficial chemical tarnish on the surface of Gold. Over time, it will build up and form a black residue. It's only superficial however, and can be easily removed. The Gold itself is unchanged.

But beholding this image now in your imagination, you don't know that, do you? All you can see is the corrupted image. Once it was pure and stunningly beautiful. Now it is filthy and encrusted with black stains.

You may open your eyes again now, but I want you to keep the memory of that image in your mind.

Despite the fact that the statue is now black and soiled, our aspirant continued to worship her — he gave her the precious flower of his youth. As time passed, the image became more and more corrupt and the aspirant found that even his conception of her had sickened.

His *conception* of her had sickened — so much so, that he very nearly abandoned his self-assigned task and threw himself back into the river.

But he did not.

13. **Then at the end appointed her body was whiter than the milk of the stars, and her lips red and warm as the sunset, and her life of a white heat like the heat of the midmost sun.**
14. **Then rose she up from the abyss of Ages of Sleep, and her body embraced me. Altogether I melted into her beauty and was glad.**

    At the "end appointed" She changed.
    Or did She?
    No, She didn't change.
    She was made of Gold, a stable, unchanging element.

Even though we first described her as a false image of the True, remember that She was made of a pure, non-corruptible substance.

In this parable, the Golden statue of Isis serves to show us the *false ideal* held by the aspirant. The Essence of the goddess is pure and true.

It was the point of view of the aspirant that was out of focus.

It was the aspirant in the boat that changed.

You must never worship any *image* of God —

You must worship the *essence* of God in the Temple of your Soul.

To his credit, our aspirant, despite being sick of heart and discouraged, continued in his Task with love under Will — Union under Will.

He didn't start out without Lust of Result. Quite the contrary.

And to make matters worse, *he adored the wrong thing for the wrong reason.* But he held fast to his *method.* Eventually, by fulfilling his Oath and Task, he became a little wiser, and his Vision passed beyond the false image of the goddess until he found himself adoring the real thing in his heart.

Years ago, one of my beloved disciples who is no longer with us, summed this up really well.

He was fond of saying, "If you pray with your lips long enough, you will eventually find yourself praying in your heart." [42]

Do you see ? That's what happened here.

This parable is also about that period of an Initiate's life that is called The Dark Night of the Soul. I wrote about it in my first book, Initiation in the Aeon of the Child, in Chapter 4, Corridors of Twilight, where I discussed The Fatal Image of Nature.

---

42   He was paraphrasing Crowley, *Book IV, Part II, Preliminary Remarks.*

Sooner or later, every serious aspirant to the Great Work will encounter the Dark Night of the Soul — the *Nigredo* or "blackness."

During that time, the Great Work itself, which you love so much, can sicken in your eyes, until you almost loathe the thought of it. Your daily practices can turn to absolute drudgery.

There is only one sure way to make it through this dreadful period. Continue in your practices with utter non-attachment — indifference. No lust of result.[43]

But you *must not* give up. You cannot leap out of that boat in mid-journey and hurl yourself back into the stream. To do that is to fail. You must do as our Prophet did; you must endure unto the end.

---

43   This practice is called वैराग्, "non-attachment." Monier-Williams, *A Sanskrit-English Dictionary*, p. 1025b.

And this Veil of Darkness will lift — I promise you. It will.

At the "end appointed" you will pass through the ordeal.

How is the end appointed?

It isn't fate, it isn't reaching a point assigned by some nebulous god or gods. Nor is it a defined period of time. It is different for everyone, based on your own individuality.

It is we, unknowingly, who set the time of the appointed end, by reason of who we are, and what we are — or even more correctly, by reason of who we are *not*, and what we are *not*.

And now in our parable, once his Vision had cleared

by the lessons of his ordeal, the aspirant then beheld Her as she *really* was — whiter than the milk of the stars. Her lips were warm and red as the sunset, like those of Hathor, goddess of the sunset and goddess of Love, she who is an eidolon of the Beauty of that Great Goddess of the stars.[44]

Her life — that is the unfolding of the Great Work in the life of the aspirant — had become a white heat, like the heat of the midday sun. Here again, is the symbolism of Tiphereth, the Sun, glowing in the heart of the aspirant — the birth of Hell.[45]

Then the goddess — symbolizing the Great Work itself — rose up out of the unconscious. She became a *conscious* component in the life of the aspirant. He "melted into her beauty" — that is, his ego was swallowed up in devotion to her.

Do you remember that the Hebrew word תפארת, *Tiphereth*, means "beauty"?

On the Tree of Life, the Sephira Tiphereth is the center of the Microcosm, the center of ourselves. We attribute the heart to Tiphereth, wherein we also attribute the Knowledge and Conversation of the Holy Guardian Angel.

---

44   Hathor, 𓉡, *ḥwt ḥr*, literally means, "mansion of Horus", sometimes translated as "house of Horus." Cf. *CDME*, p. 166 and Wilkinson, *The Complete Gods and Goddesses of Ancient Egypt*, pp. 139-145.

45   See Gunther, *The Parable of the New Birth*, pp. 37-38.

15. The river also became the river of Amrit, and the little boat was the chariot of the flesh, and the sails thereof the blood of the heart that beareth me, that beareth me.
16. O serpent woman of the stars! I, even I, have fashioned Thee from a pale image of fine gold.

And with this, our humble aspirant realized that the river upon which he traveled was the *River of Amrit* — the River of Immortality.[46] The little boat is his own body. He calls it the chariot of what? The chariot of the flesh.

It is perhaps significant that this Parable occurs in the second Chapter of Liber LXV wherein the first two Verses read,

> **I passed into the mountain of lapis-lazuli, even as a green hawk between the pillars of turquoise that is seated upon the throne of the East.**
> **So came I to Duant, the starry abode, and I heard voices crying aloud.**

In the ancient Egyptian text called *The Book of what is in the Duat* the boat that carried the sun god was called 𓇋𓄹𓏤, *iwf,* which means "flesh."[47] In Liber LXV likewise, the

---

46 In Sanskrit, अमृत, Monier-Williams, *A Sanskrit-English Dictionary*, p. 82b.

47 For *iwf,* see CDME p. 13. See also Hornung, *The Egyptian Amduat*, First Hour, Middle Register 46 (p. 24).

vessel for the journey through the *Duat*, the Starry Abode, is the boat of flesh.⁴⁸

And those purple sails formed to catch the fair wind of Divine Inspiration? They are the very blood of his heart.⁴⁹ In other words, the Divine Inspiration of God that he sought to capture was in him — all the time.

There is no god but man.

And he cries out an adoration, at last, to the *True Essence of the goddess, the serpent woman of the stars,* almost in disbelief at what has occurred — "I, even I, have fashioned Thee from a pale image of fine gold."

Who is the "serpent woman of the stars"? It is the goddess ⚬⌒𓏤, *nwt*, Nuit. The goddess of the starry night. In *The Book of the Law* she says, "I am Infinite Space, and the Infinite Stars thereof..."⁵⁰ Note the use of the upper case letters in mid-sentence in this phrase: *Infinite Space, Infinite Stars*. I.S.I.S.

In the ancient Egyptian hieroglyphics, Her name was also written, ⚬⌒𓆙, with the determinative of the Cobra;⁵¹

---

48   The spelling of "Duat" as "Duant" in Liber LXV may be a purely poetic expression. This is uncertain.

49   He sails upon the blood of the River of Life, which is the collective stream of all humankind. The blood of the heart is an individual stream, unique to each person.

50   *Liber AL* I:22.

51   BM 10470, *Papyrus of Any,* I,7 (sheet 5.) A variation, spelled ⚬⌒𓆙, occurs in this same Papyrus in a version of BD 15, 3 (sheet 19).

indeed, she is the serpent woman of the stars.[52]

As aspirants to the Great Work, our initial conceptions of Truth are always pale images of the real thing. But it is what we have. And we have to make the best of it. In the 17th Aethyr of *The Vision & The Voice*, we are told this in no uncertain terms.

"Your falsehood is but a little falser than your truth.
Yet by your truth, shall ye come to Truth."

We must formulate our idea of truth, and hold fast to it at all costs. However, remember that it is but the *pale image* of the actual Truth.

Note carefully the use of upper-case letters in this quote from *The Vision & The Voice*. In each instance, "your truth" is written with a lower-case "t", while the final "Truth" has an upper-case "T." Because our "truth" is such a pale image, our "falsehood" is only a little falser than our "truth." From our human, non-initiated perspective, it is but a "little truth."

But if we endure unto the end, by means of this little truth, we will arrive at the Great Truth — Truth written with an upper case "T."

Take heart my brothers and sisters.

---

52 The phrase "serpent woman" only appears here, in this verse. The word "serpent-woman" occurs in Liber LXV, 3:5, but there it is hyphenated to indicate a single compound word.

Even I, and you, may fashion the serpent woman of the stars from a pale image of fine gold.

In the name of the Lord of Initiation, Amen.
Love is the law, love under will.

The Parable
of the
Hummingbird

Liber LXV, Chapter 5, verses 52-56

LECTURE SERIES VOL. 1

PARABLES OF THELEMA
Part III

THE PARABLE OF THE HUMMINGBIRD

Liber LXV, Chapter 5, verses 52-56

Title Page Art: "ere the moon waxed thrice" by Annette Eustace Gray

ναρθηκοφόροι μὲν πολλοί,
βάκχοι δέ τε παῦροι.

List of Illustrations

p. 120	'Hummingbird Collecting Nectar,' *Depositphotos.*
p. 121	'Hummingbird Collecting Nectar,' *Depositphotos.*
p. 123	'Variis Trochilieæ,' Annette Eustace Gray.
p. 125	'From flower to flower,' Annette Eustace Gray.
p. 126	'Simple Simon,' *Denslow's Mother Goose, (1901 e.v.)*
p. 129	'Horned cerastes,' Annette Eustace Gray.
p. 133	'Cerastes Cornatus,' *Zoology of Egypt, Vol. 1, Reptilia and Batrachia, Plate XLVIII (1898 e.v.)*
P. 134	'prayed him for poison,' Annette Eustace Gray.
p. 135	'the royal Uræus serpent, answered him....,' Annette Eustace Gray.
p. 136	'Naja Haje,' *Zoology of Egypt, Vol. 1, Reptilia and Batrachia, Plate XLIV (1898 e.v.)*
p. 137	'Pharoah Sety I,' *Denkmäler aus Ägypten und Äthiopien, Abth. III, Bl. 296.*
p. 139	'Serpent spitting fire in the faces of the enemies of Osiris,' *The Book of Pylons, Ninth Hour, lower register. Sarcophogus of Sety I.*
p. 139	'Naja Haje,' *Dictionnaire universel d'historie naturelle, Vol. 2 Atlas (1847 e.v.)*
p. 141	'The god Nun lifting the Bark of the Newborn Sun from the Waters of Chaos,'

	The Egyptian Book of the Dead. Facsimiles of the Papyri of Hunefer, Anhai, Kerasher and Netchemet Papyrus of Anhai, Plate 9. (1899 e.v.)
p. 143	'Ra in the Boat of Millions (of years),' *The Egyptian Book of the Dead. The Papyrus of Ani, Plate 22* (1894 e.v.)
p. 144	'The god Geb,' *The Gods of the Egyptians, Vol. 2, Plate 19* (1904 e.v.)
p. 149	'The Visit of Nicodemus,' John La Farge (1890 e.v.), Smithsonian American Art Museum.
p. 153	'an Ibis that meditated upon the bank,' *Annette Eustace Gray.*
p. 154	'The god Thoth,' *Panthéon égyptien collection des personnages* (1823 e.v.)
p. 155	'Hapy of the North & South,' *Denkmäler aus Ägypten und Äthiopien, Abth. V, Bl 13.*
p. 157	'generations of my children,' *Annette Eustace Gray.*
p. 158	'Sacred Ibis,' *A History of Birds of Europe, Not Observed in the British Isles, Vol. 4, Plate 45* (1863 e.v.)
p. 161	'Ibis Religiosa,' *The Beautiful and Curious Birds of the World, Plate 19* (1883 e.v.)

THE PARABLE OF THE HUMMINGBIRD

Do what thou wilt shall be the whole of the Law.

Once again, I would like to discuss a Parable from the Holy Books. This parable is found in Liber LXV, Chapter 5, verses 52-56.

I call it, "The Parable of the Hummingbird."

Let's begin by reading the text of these Verses:

52. There was also an humming-bird that spake unto the horned cerastes, and prayed him for poison. And the great snake of Khem the Holy One, the royal Uræus serpent, answered him and said:

53. I sailed over the sky of Nu in the car called Millions-of-Years, and I saw not any creature upon Seb that was equal to me. The venom of my fang is the inheritance of my father, and of my father's father; and how shall I give it unto thee? Live thou and thy children as I and my fathers have lived, even unto an hundred millions of generations, and it may be that the mercy of the Mighty Ones may bestow upon thy children a drop of the poison of eld.

54. Then the humming-bird was afflicted in his spirit, and

he flew unto the flowers, and it was as if naught had been spoken between them. Yet in a little while a serpent struck him that he died.

55. But an Ibis that meditated upon the bank of Nile the beautiful god listened and heard. And he laid aside his Ibis ways, and became as a serpent, saying Peradventure in an hundred millions of millions of generations of my children, they shall attain to a drop of the poison of the fang of the Exalted One.

56. And behold! ere the moon waxed thrice he became an Uræus serpent, and the poison of the fang was established in him and his seed even for ever and for ever.

This has always been my favorite parable in The Holy Books. It is exquisitely conceived, beautifully written and wonderfully lucid.

Now, audience participation time again:

Someone please name all the characters of this parable — anyone?

Thank you. Some say three, some say four. Let's see who was correct, shall we?

Crowley called this the *Parable of the Ibis, the Hummingbird, and the Uræus serpent*. I have chosen the shorter title of *The Parable of the Hummingbird* only for convenience.

There are *three basic points of view* expressed in this lovely Parable.

First, the attitude of the hummingbird, the first major character in this little tale.

Secondly, the Divine Nature expressed by the Uræus serpent.

Lastly, the inspirational and admirable attitude of the Ibis.[1]

They all intertwine to impart unto us a valuable instruction — an instruction that all of us should study carefully.

But — and this is important — there are not just three characters in this Parable. There are four.

More on this later. But let's continue on our examination of the Parable.

To begin with, I would like for us to examine the character of the hummingbird. If we study this carefully, we will discover some interesting facts that will help with the exegesis of these verses.

By the way, this is a technique that I strongly advise

---

[1] The word "humming-bird" is written with an initial Lower Case letter and a hyphen in the Class A text of Liber LXV. In the title of this commentary, "Hummingbird" is capitalized for *emphasis only*, and the modern spelling is used in preference to the archaic spelling with the hyphen. The words "Uræus" and "Ibis" are written with initial Upper Case letters in the Class A text in contradistinction to "humming-bird" with the lower case initial letter. This distinction in the Sacred Text should be considered significant. The ligature "æ" in "Uræus" is an archaic typesetting convention only, not required to maintain fidelity to the original text of Liber LXV. It is regrettable that we do not possess the original handwritten manuscript.

with any of The Holy Books — do not take any symbol or reference for granted. Examine it in detail. There is always a wealth of information there — tucked away inside a simple reference may be a treasure-trove of instruction that will be missed if you don't take the time to look.

For example, when you read this verse — ask yourself, why a hummingbird? Why not a sparrow or a crow? Well, let's see if we can find out why.

Now the first fact I want all of you to consider is this: hummingbirds only exist in North, Central and South America.[2] Fossils of ancient hummingbirds that are 30 million years old have been found in Europe, so we know that one time they lived there.[3] But they became extinct in that region millions of years ago. The honey-eaters of Australia are similar in some regards, but they are not hummingbirds. There are no hummingbirds in Australia or Europe or Asia.

What I find really interesting is this:

---

2   Hanson, *World of Hummingbirds*, p. v.

3   Mayr, *Fossil Hummingbirds of the Old World*, in *The Biologist*, 52, No. 1, (2005) pp. 12-15.

Hummingbirds do not exist in Africa either. Hummingbirds therefore do not exist in Egypt. They never have.

The Hummingbird

So why is a hummingbird having a conversation with the royal Uraeus serpent of Khem? Because this is a Parable, not a lesson in Ornithology or Geography! And because it is a Parable, it has license to break those rules for the sake of symbolism. And the meaning of each of these characters is vitally important to this lesson.

So, let's take a look at the hummingbird. For those of you who haven't had the pleasure of ever seeing one in nature, you've really missed something.

They are exquisitely beautiful, tiny little birds. A grown man could easily put one of them in the palm of his hand. Their average length is about 3 inches or 7.6 centimeters. There are some a bit larger, but most of them are quite small.

The number of species of hummingbird is very large, and they are extremely varied in color — their feathers often exhibit metallic colors of gold and silver, as well as the hues of just about every precious stone imaginable.

Hummingbirds have the ability to hover in one place in the air, their wings flapping at such a rate of speed they appear only as a colored blur. They are the only bird known that has the ability to fly backwards. They flit from flower to flower, searching for nectar and insects almost constantly.

At any given time, a hummingbird is only hours away from starving to death because of the energy they burn in flying. They have the highest in-flight metabolism of any bird in the world. They have to eat one and a half times their body weight in nectar or small insects every day in order to maintain their energy requirements.[4]

During the night, in order to survive, they are capable of entering into a state of torpor where the systems of their

---

4   Williamson, *A Field Guide to Hummingbirds of North America*, p.19.

body slow down to a point near death.[5] A hummingbird in a state of torpor shows no lung activity, appears to have no heart-beat, and when touched, shows no signs of life at all. They will reliably awaken from this torpor about two hours before sunrise on cue from some internal circadian clock.

Then, they begin their frenzied feeding cycle once again.

Another little fact about hummingbirds — they are ill-tempered little buggers. They are one of the most aggressive birds known. They not only quarrel with each other, but will not hesitate to attack a much larger bird intruding on their territory. They have also been observed attacking chipmunks and squirrels.

As a brief aside, I want to mention a curious incident. While I was writing these passages, a hummingbird flew into our house from an open door! It flew frantically around our ceiling, completely disoriented. We had to wait until the poor thing grew so tired that it finally came to rest atop our curtains. My wife Gwen was then able to gently capture the exhausted bird in a soft cloth and take it outside.

Why do I mention this? This is clearly an example of *Synchronicity*. The analytical psychologist Carl Jung used the term to designate simultaneous circumstances which appear to be meaningfully related, but have no causal connection.

---

5   *Ibid.* p. 22. They will also become torpid in extreme cold weather, or times of insufficient food.

In this instance, it just happened to be a hummingbird. I'm just glad it wasn't a snake! But I digress.

So, in this Parable, who or what does the hummingbird represent?

It represents a certain type of would-be aspirant. I say **would-be** because most of the ones who are like the hummingbird **won't-be**.

Just take the characteristic of the hummingbird to flit from flower to flower.

I've seen would-be aspirants like that many times in my life.

They seem to be attracted to the realms of the spiritual in one way or another, but they flit from here to there, trying to sample the wares of every vendor in the market — good, bad or mediocre.

They are willing to taste the goods, but don't want to pay any price for them.

Most of you know the nursery rhyme of *Simple Simon*, don't you? The implicit moral of this little rhyme is a perfect description of this type of would-be aspirant.

"Simple Simon met a pieman,
Going to the fair;
Says Simple Simon to the pieman,
'Let me taste your ware.'
Says the pie-man to Simple Simon,
'Show me first your penny.'
Says Simple Simon to the pieman,
'Indeed I have not any.'

Simple Simon went a-fishing
For to catch a whale:
All the water he had got
Was in his mother's pail."[6]

Aspirants like Simple Simon want a taste of the pie — but are unable to pay the penny should they like it, and unwilling to work to acquire that penny.

They dream of catching whales in a mop bucket.

Many years ago, I received a call from a friend who asked if I would bring my deck of Tarot Cards and come over to her house. She had a friend that she wanted me to meet, to introduce him to Tarot and Qabalah.

Well, I was very young then, in my early twenties, and naive in the ways of these things. So I went.

I met the young man, and all of us sat on the parlor floor as I set about explaining the basics of Tarot. I began to explain how the cards have Zodiacal, Planetary and Elemental attributions, and have Qabalistic correspondences. Then I began to tell him that it was just a tool of my Spiritual School.

He stopped me abruptly. He had heard all he wanted to hear.

He actually told me, "Look, I want to be cool with *Jesus* and *Buddha* and *Krishna*, I just don't want to do anything

---

[6] *Denslow's Mother Goose, Being the Old Familiar Rhymes and Jingles of Mother Goose.*

that would piss any of them off! These Tarot cards are cool, but man — there's a lot of them! It would take a lot of work to learn all that! Besides, why should I listen to you? You are not any older than me."

With that, he promptly got up, thanked our mutual friend, and went on his way.

Some years later, he was still looking at other flowers. The last I heard of him he was poking his nose into *The Urantia Book* — and still trying not to piss off Jesus or Buddha or Krishna.[7]

In over forty years he hasn't been able to commit himself to a single thing. Not one.

52. **There was also an humming-bird that spake unto the horned cerastes, and prayed him for poison. And the great snake of Khem the Holy One, the royal Uræus serpent, answered him…**

The Horned Cerastes

Now, at the very beginning of our Parable, we see the hummingbird begging for poison. To whom did he address his plea?

---

7   *The Urantia Book* is a lengthy anonymous book supposedly written by celestial beings. It claims to possess the true knowledge of the origin and meaning of life, mankind's relationship to God, the life of Jesus, along with assorted pseudo-mystical mumbo-jumbo.

The horned cerastes — not the Uræus serpent.

The hummingbird went to the horned cerastes, a venomous viper of Egypt, and asked to possess the poison of the serpent.[8]

When I first read this verse many years ago, I missed a fascinating little detail. But once I became a serious student of Egyptology, it jumped off the page. First of all, the hummingbird isn't speaking to the Uræus at all — he is talking to a horned cerastes — *another snake altogether*. When I first read this verse, in my haste I made the erroneous assumption that the horned cerastes and the Uræus were the same.

How many of you here made that assumption? Let's

---

8   The name "cerastes" is derived from the Greek κεράστης, "horned." (*LSJ* p. 941b).

see a show of hands. Some of you missed that, didn't you? Just like I did years ago.

But secondly, as a student of Egyptian Hieroglyphics, this also meant something quite specific to me. The horned cerastes, or horned viper, is one of the characters in the ancient Egyptian hieroglyphic alphabet:

It is used phonetically for the letter "*f*." [9] One might wonder why the horned cerastes was chosen to signify the phonetic sound of the letter "*f*."[10]

Egyptologist Alan Gardiner noted that, "It is curious how often the consonant '*f*' appears in words for snake..." By this, he meant , *wfỉ,* an ancient word from the *Pyramid Texts,* as well as , *fnṯ,* , *ḥfȝw*, and , *ḏdft,* later words which can all have the generic sense of "snake."[11]

He further took particular notice of , *ḏdft,* which he suggested was a compound word meaning, "*which says fff.*"[12] The latter portion of the word is attested in *Demotic* as a name for the *cerastes viper,* , *fy*.[13]

---

9   See Gardiner, *Egyptian Grammar*, p. 476.

10 Gardiner, *Ancient Egyptian Onomasitca,* Vol. 2, 69*.

11 For *wfỉ*, see *PT* 419c (Allen 278 (W), 3); for *fnṯ, ḥfȝw* and *ḏdft* see CDME pp. 98, 168 & 326.

12 Composed of the verb , *ḏd*, "say, speak", plus , "*f*" as a phoneme only, not a suffix-pronoun. CDME p 326 & Allen 2.3. It was probably pronounced "*ḏdf,*" vocalized as "*čed-eff.*" The feminine ending "*t*" would have been silent.

13 Erichsen, *Demotisches Glossar*, p. 144. This word is to be read right-to-left.

Writing in *The Journal of Egyptian Archaeology*, Percy Newberry referenced Gardiner's note, and added, "This is precisely the sound the cerastes (*Cerastus cornatus*)...emits when at bay, and ever since I first encountered vipers (in 1891) I have regarded the name *fy* as onomatopœic."[14]

The cerastes, when threatened, will rub its rough keeled scales together very rapidly, making a rasping sound[15] like "*ffffff*", hence the phonetic sound of "*f*."

But more importantly — and this is what struck me so many years ago — is that the hieroglyphic character of the horned cerastes is used grammatically as a *suffix pronoun*. It is the *Third Person Masculine Singular Pronoun* meaning, "He, Him, His, It or Its."[16]

To illustrate this, I have translated a latter portion of this parable into Middle Egyptian for you. Here it is: "A serpent struck him that he died."

| *dm sw* | *ḥf3w* | *r* | *mt.n=f* |
| Struck him | a serpent | that | died he. |

Ancient Egyptian was a verbal language, meaning the

---

14   Newberry, *The Journal of Egyptian Archaeology*, Vol. 34 (1948), p. 118.

15   Department of the Navy, *Poisonous Snakes of the World*, P. 83. Cf. Anderson, *Zoology of Egypt, Vol. 1*, p. 333.

16   CDME, p. 97.

verb typically initiates a sentence. Here you see how the suffix pronoun "ƒ", signifying "him" or "he", is appended to the final verb in this sentence: *mt.n=f,* "died he."

I found it most interesting that the image of the poisonous snake our hummingbird approached is used as the letter which indicates *a personal pronoun.*

He. Belonging to *him.* Pertaining to *him.* His.[17]
Can we derive a meaningful suggestion from that?
Perhaps, but let's wait and see.

The common Egyptian word for "serpent" or "snake" specifically meant the *"horned cerastes,"* and was written in hieroglyphics as ⟨hieroglyphs⟩, *ḥfꜣw (hefau).* That same word is written in Coptic as ϩⲟϥ, *"hof",* which is probably very close to how it was really pronounced.[18] I use Coptic fairly often to amplify some Egyptian words because Coptic was the final development in the Egyptian Language.

Sometimes it can give us a clue to the actual pronunciation of an ancient Egyptian word. At times

---

17   It can also signify the third person masculine "it"or "its." See above, footnote 16.

18   *Vycichl,* p. 319b. *Crum,* p. 740b. This is in the Sahidic and Boharic dialects. It translates the Greek ὄφις, "serpent", which is very similar in pronunciation. Cf. Hebrew אפעה, *ef 'eh,* Arabic أفعى, *'afeaa,* "viper" (*Gesenius,* p. 72a) and Amharic አፉኝት, *affuññut,* "viper" (Kane, *Amharic-English Dictionary,* Vol. 2, p. 1358b).

it suggests more subtle meanings that we might not see otherwise.

This language is still read aloud in Coptic churches to this day. It's the closest thing you will ever hear to what the ancient Egyptian language really sounded like.

So, *hefau* is the most common word used to indicate "serpent" in Middle Egyptian.[19] Do you see? That is the same word I used in our Egyptian sentence for "a serpent." When the ancient Egyptians used this word, they were thinking of a very common snake in their area, the poisonous viper — the horned cerastes. Now, while the bite of a cerastes is dangerous, it rarely is fatal to humans because the venom

---

19   For *ḥfꜣw,* see CDME, p. 168.

is normally only mildly toxic.[20] But to small animals and birds, it is deadly.

Nevertheless, the hummingbird brazenly approached the horned cerastes and prayed him for poison.

Here is another interesting point.

The horned cerastes does not climb trees; it is a snake of the desert, and rocks. However, it is sometimes found in an *Oasis*.[21]

So, in our little myth, let's visualize a hummingbird

---

20   Department of Defense, *Venomous Snakes of the Middle East*, pp. 17-21.

21   *Ibid.* p. 17.

flitting about an oasis near the Nile river, with various flowers all about, and he spies the horned cerastes, relaxing under a date palm tree.

And the hummingbird envied the ancient venom of the serpent, and he prayed him for his poison.

Now this doesn't mean that he wanted a little bit of the poison to take with him like nectar — he wanted to be able to *generate* that venom in the manner of the serpent.

He was envious of it. He wanted it. He wanted to be *like* the serpent.

The request of the hummingbird is promptly answered — but not by our little horned cerastes to whom he addressed the question — but by the royal Uræus serpent, the great snake of Khem[22] — an emblem of royalty, divinity and divine authority in ancient Egypt.[23]

The little horned cerastes never utters a word.

The Uræus Serpent

The word "Uræus" is derived from the Greek word οὐραῖος which means, "on its tail."[24] In Egyptian Arabic they call it أورايوس, *ur'ius*, which is just an Arabic pronunciation of the Greek/English word.

This Greek word, in turn, came from the ancient

---

22   "Khem" is 𓆎𓅓𓏏𓊖 , *kmt*, "the Black Land," that is, "Egypt." *CDME*, p. 286.

23   Frankfort, *Kingship and the Gods*, p. 131.

24   From οὐρά, "tail" (*LSJ*, p. 1272b).

Egyptian ![hieroglyph], *i'rt,* meaning, "rearing cobra."²⁵ We know from the ancient texts and monuments of ancient Egypt that the Uræus represented the *cobra*.

The Uræus signified royalty *par excellence* in Egypt. It adorned the brows of Pharoahs as an imposing symbol of ruling power, as well as serving as magical protection for the Pharoah himself. However, when referring to the Uræus serpent as a deity and protectress of the gods, and guardian upon the diadem of a King, the Egyptians used the word ![hieroglyph], *ȝḫt, akhet,* an epithet meaning "glorious one."²⁶

---

25   *CDME, p.* 11. The phonetic "t" that ends the word indicates that it is a feminine noun. It was probably not pronounced. Cf. *The New Shorter Oxford English Dictionary* (1993), Vol.2, p.3527.

26   Or "splendid one." *CDME, p.* 4. The word *ȝḫt* is feminine, hence it is sometime translated as "Cobra-goddess."

In *The Book of the Dead*, Spell 15Bii, it is recounted how the Uræus had risen to defend *Ra-Hoor-Khuit*, enabling him to repel the fiend *Apep*, enemy of the sun-god:

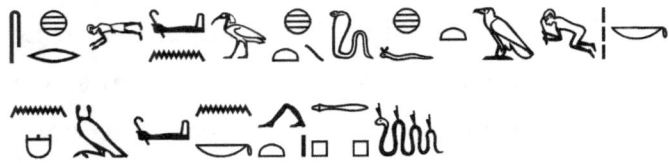

"*The Uræus has overthrown thine enemies!
Thou hast checked the advance of Apep!*" ²⁷

Here, in this word , *ȝḫt*, akhet, there is also clearly a connection between the words , *ȝḫt*, "the eye (of a god)" and , *ȝḫt*, "flame."²⁸

The Pharoahs believed that, as manifestations of the sun god *Ra*, they were protected by the Uræus serpent-goddess, who would spit fire upon their enemies. In actual fact, the spitting cobra rears into an erect posture with its hood spread menacingly and spits its venom up to 12 feet, *directly at the eyes* of its enemy.²⁹

---

27   *sḫr.n ȝḫt ḫftyw=k / nḥm.n=k nmt ʿȝpp.* Line 2 reads literally, "*Thou hast seized the step of Apep.*" (Dublin Papyrus 1661).

28   *CDME, pp.* 4-5.

29   Cochran, *Poisonous Reptiles of the World,* p.28. Some species of the Cobra (*naja naja*) are "spitting Cobras," while others are not. The Egyptians did not appear to distinguish between them.

Thus, it is no surprise to us that the one who declares the mystery of the "poison of eld"[30] is not the little horned cerastes originally addressed by the hummingbird, but the serpent that signified the royal land of Egypt itself — the royal Uræus serpent.

---

30   "eld" means "old age, antiquity." Now considered an obsolete word, it was once common. It is etymologically linked to the word "old." (*Skeat* 186b-187a).

The Poison of Eld

52. There was also an humming-bird that spake unto the horned cerastes, and prayed him for poison. And the great snake of Khem the Holy One, the royal Uræus serpent, answered him and said:

53. I sailed over the sky of Nu in the car called Millions-of-Years, and I saw not any creature upon Seb that was equal to me. The venom of my fang is the inheritance of my father, and of my father's father; and how shall I give it unto thee? Live thou and thy children as I and my fathers have lived, even unto an hundred millions of generations, and it may be that the mercy of the Mighty Ones may bestow upon thy children a drop of the poison of eld.

The royal Uræus first told the hummingbird that he had sailed over the sky of Nu in the car called "Millions-of-Years."

Now, let's get our Egyptology straight here before we go any further.

The "Nu" mentioned here has nothing whatsoever to do with the "Nu" mentioned in *The Book of The Law*.

This spelling of "Nu" in Liber LXV refers to [hieroglyphs], the primeval watery abyss.

Egyptologists now render this word as *nwn,* that is, "*nun.*" [31]

---

[31] Crowley's knowledge of Egyptology was minimal. There is incontrovertible evidence that he used the 1898 publication of Budge's synoptic *The Book of the Dead, The Chapters of Coming Forth by Day,* as

This was the source of the Coptic word ⲚⲞⲨⲚ, *nun*, *"the abyss."*³² The primeval waters called *nun* signified the source from whence all things arose and it was the great ocean of the heavens whereon the boat of Ra traveled daily.³³ Thus, the "sky of Nu" here represents the eternal ocean of the *dawn*.³⁴

How do we know it refers to the morning?

We know that because the verse tells us that the royal serpent was sailing the sky of Nu in the car called "Millions-of-Years."³⁵

---

well as Budge's 1895 publication *The Book of the Dead, The Papyrus of Ani*. In the latter, for example on page *cvii*, the name of the primeval watery mass is spelled "Nu." Budge continued to use this spelling long after it had been proven incorrect. (Cf. *An Egyptian Hieroglyphic Dictionary* (1920), Vol. 1, p. 349.) The German Egyptologist Adolph Erman had already established that the correct transliteration was *nun* by the time of his publication *Aegypten und Aegyptisches Leben im Altertum* in 1885. (Translated into English in 1894 as *Life in Ancient Egypt*).

32   Vycichl, p.143b.

33   Wilkinson, *The Complete Gods and Goddesses of Ancient Egypt*, p. 117.

34   It is entirely likely that Crowley confused "Nun" with the spelling of "Nuit" as "Nu" in *The Book of the Law*.

35   The etymology of "car" is connected with "carry, cart, chariot" and many other words, but ultimately deriving from the Sanskrit चर्, *car*, "to move." (Skeat p. 93b, Monier-Williams, *A Sanskrit-English Dictionary*, p.389a).

In Egyptian hieroglyphics, the words 𓅓𓏤𓊪𓈖𓎛𓎛, *wiꜣ n ḥḥ*, (*wia en heh*), meant "the boat of millions (of years)."[36] It was another name for 𓅓𓂝𓈖𓆓𓏏, *mꜥndt*, (*mandjet*), the "bark of the dawn."[37] So, we know the mighty Uræus serpent sailed over the primeval waters with Ra at dawn, viewing the earth below.

This time of day is important, because in ancient Egyptian symbolism the dawn signified *birth and resurrection* — in other words, *life*.

The bark called "millions of years" is not merely the boat of the sun god that carries him on his daily voyage across the sky. It represents *life* in an endless cycle — new lives and recurring lives — generation after generation after generation.

The concept of generation.

---

36   *Wb* I, p. 271.

37   *CDME*, p. 105.

53. I sailed over the sky of Nu in the car called Millions-of-Years, and I saw not any creature upon Seb that was equal to me.

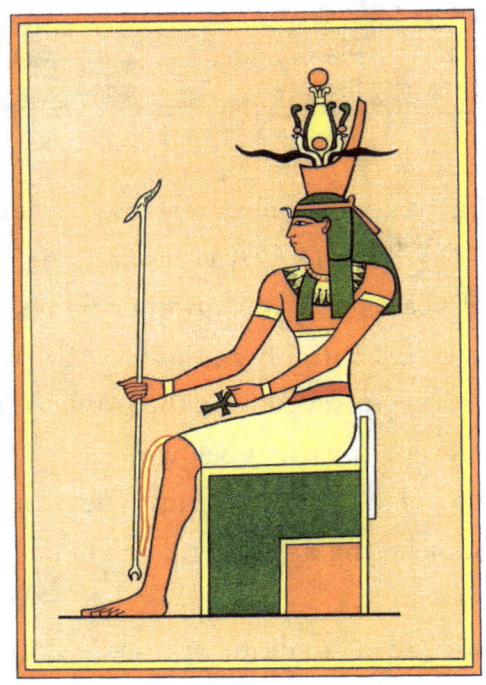

So, the royal Uræus serpent has told the hummingbird that for generation after generation after generation, "I saw not any creature upon Seb that was equal to me."

Now, once again, let's get our Egyptology straight very quickly.

In the early days of Egyptology the name of the Egyptian god of earth 𓅭𓃀𓀭, *gb,* was translated as "*Seb.*" At the time these verses came to be written, that was the name known to Aleister Crowley from reading the books of

E. A. Wallis Budge. That is why it takes that form in Liber LXV. Egyptologists would come to learn that the name of this god was actually "*Geb.*"[38]

As an aside, do you remember that the *Gnomes* are the Elementals of Earth? Can anybody here tell me the name of the king of the Gnomes? Anyone?

Yes, that's right. It was *Gob*.[39] His subjects were sometimes called *Goblins*. Isn't the similarity of those two words interesting? Do any of you think that there is a very old connection there? Yes, I believe there actually is a connection.

The ancient Egyptian god of earth is *Geb*; the king of the Elementals of Earth is *Gob*.

I just find that curious and interesting. But I digress.

53. I sailed over the sky of Nu in the car called Millions-of-Years, and I saw not any creature upon Seb that was equal to me. The venom of my fang is the inheritance of my father, and of my father's father; and how shall I give it unto thee?

---

38 Adolph Erman had already published the correct translation of *Geb* by 1904 e.v. in his *Aegyptisches Glossar*. E.A. Wallis Budge used "Seb" in *The Gods of the Egyptians* in that same year. He continued to use the outdated "Seb" as late as 1911 e.v. in the new revised and enlarged edition of *Books on Egypt and Chaldea*, Vol. 31, *A Hieroglyphic Vocabulary to the Theban Rescension of The Book of the Dead*.

39 See Eliphas Levi (trans. Waite), *Transcendental Magic*, p. 221. Sometimes spelled "Ghob" (see 777, Col. LXII).

The Uræus told the witless hummingbird that the sacred poison cannot be given away as if it were a Christmas present. The royal serpent was the custodian of an elixir passed through his bloodline for generations upon end.

And when he said, "and how shall I give it unto thee?", he was saying, "Look, you are a bird, not a snake. How can I give this to you?"

53. ... The venom of my fang is the inheritance of my father, and of my father's father; and how shall I give it unto thee? Live thou and thy children as I and my fathers have lived, even unto an hundred millions of generations, and it may be that the mercy of the Mighty Ones may bestow upon thy children a drop of the poison of eld.

If you want to experience the precious gifts granted unto the Initiate, then you must *be* an Initiate. I tell this to my disciples all the time. If you want to be an Initiate, start acting like one.

When my own dear mother thought that I wasn't behaving as a young gentleman should behave, she used to chastise me by saying, "Act like you *are* somebody!"

If you call yourself an Initiate, you need to act like one.

If you want to become an Adept of the A∴A∴, you have to start as a Probationer. If you want to be a Zelator, you first have to be a Neophyte. You have to learn to crawl before you walk, and learn to walk before you run.

I wrote about this in my first book *Initiation in the Aeon of the Child,* in Chapter 3, "Two Horizons."

All too often students want to daydream of Work far beyond their means and beyond their Oaths, rather than concentrating patiently on the basics.

It's natural to desire greater attainment. And while the goal is *tomorrow*, the road that leads there is always *today*.

This, I believe, is one of the great lessons of Thelema — you must tend to the *here and now*, for this is the foundation upon which your future is formulated.

Start at the beginning and endure until the end.

Several years ago, the leadership of the A∴A∴ was approached by an intelligent young man who was a senior member in a well-known group that presents itself as the A∴A∴. He came to ask what he had to do to become a member of what he called "the real A∴A∴" (his words, not mine), because he had come to believe that he had been fooled and that the group that he had joined didn't represent the A∴A∴ at all.

This young man was told that he had to start over as a Probationer because the people that had given him all of his Grades had no Authority at all in the eyes of the A∴A∴, and it would be impossible to determine by what criteria they had evaluated his previous work.

He accepted that judgement graciously, because he knew in his heart it was the right thing to do. As an honorable man, he immediately went to the leader of that group and told her in person that he was leaving and why. Then he walked away from that leader as she wept bitter tears.

He went on to fulfill the Task of Probationer and was Initiated as a Neophyte in the A∴A∴.

Shortly thereafter, another senior member of that group followed the same course of action. He also fulfilled the Task of Probationer and was Initiated as a Neophyte.

They instinctively understood the message of the Uraeus serpent in this Parable. They desired the True Elixir, not a pale imitation, and they had the courage to admit they had been wrong, and to seek out the right way.

And these two gentlemen were not the only ones. There have been others, men and women, who have courageously done the same thing.

But the little hummingbird couldn't do that. The answer he received wasn't what he wanted to hear.

54. **Then the humming-bird was afflicted in his spirit, and he flew unto the flowers, and it was as if naught had been spoken between them. Yet in a little while a serpent struck him that he died.**

He was "afflicted in his spirit" to hear this.

The word "afflicted" means to be grievously affected or troubled. The etymology of "afflicted" tells us that its original meaning was, "to strike to the ground."[40]

---

40   *Skeat* p. 11a.

This reminds me of a modern expression we have when someone experiences a serious deflation. We say, "It knocked the wind right out of them."

So, our little bird just flew off into the flowers as if the conversation, and the reason for it, had never taken place.

In addition to the type of aspirants that I mentioned before, who had the courage to right their wrongs and start over, there has been the occasional hummingbird.

Another member of that same group came to the leadership of the A∴A∴ secretly, rather like Nicodemus who came to see Jesus by night so that he could not be seen.[41]

---
41   *The Gospel of John* 3:1-2.

You see, Nicodemus was a Pharisee and a member of the powerful Sanhedrin.[42] He had been deeply moved by the accounts he had heard of Jesus, and he felt the need to speak to him directly. But if he did so, he couldn't risk being seen by his peers because Jesus was a very controversial figure and threatened the status-quo.

Nicodemus went to Jesus because he believed him to be a genuine holy man sent by God. The text of the New Testament does not record what Nicodemus *wanted* to hear, but from the answer he received, one can only deduce that he wanted to know what he must do in order to experience the Kingdom of God:

> ἀπεκρίθη Ἰησοῦς καὶ εἶπεν αὐτῷ Ἀμὴν ἀμὴν λέγω σοι, ἐὰν μή τις γεννηθῇ ἄνωθεν, οὐ δύναται ἰδεῖν τὴν Βασιλείαν τοῦ θεοῦ.
>
> *"Jesus answered him and said unto him, Truly, truly I say unto thee. Unless one is born again, he is not able to see the Kingdom of God."*[43]

This deeply troubled Nicodemus. He was troubled about who he was and what he was doing. He desired the truth, but you see, he was afraid of the consequences should he turn from his former ways.

---

42   "Sanhedrin," the supreme council of the Jews. The word is derived from the Greek συνέδριον, "assembly," in turn from the Aramaic סנהדרין (Jastrow, *A Dictionary of the Tarbumim, the Talmud Bibli and Yerushalmi, and the Midrashic Literature*, Vol. 2, p. 1005, a-b.).

43   *The Gospel of John*, 3:3.

And so it was with this other member of that group falsely calling itself A∴ A∴. He came secretly by night and asked how he could regularize his aspiration to the A∴ A∴.

If you will pardon my analogy, he was told that he had to be "born again." He was told that he had to start over.

Well, our modern day little Nicodemus didn't want to hear that. He went back to the group that he knew to be false and took up his old life, as if naught had been spoken between us.

He became one of the highest ranking members of that group. But the members of his group, to this day, do not know of his secret rendezvous by night so long ago. They do not know that his real name should be "Nicodemus."

Some birds find it better to reign in hell than serve in heaven.[44]

So too, it was with our little hummingbird. He flew into the flowers and pretended the conversation never took place. And in a little while, a serpent struck him that he died.

Now, what serpent was it that killed him? Was it the Uræus?

No. Our little bird had flown away into the flowers — in other words, he returned to his former life that he lived prior to asking the troubling question.

---

44   This paraphrase is based on the monologue by Satan in John Milton's *The Paradise Lost*, Book I, Line 262.

Was it our little mute horned cerastes? I think so, and I'll tell you why.

Do you know what I think? I think that the hummingbird self-destructed.

Remember the sentence from this Parable that I translated into Egyptian earlier in this lecture? Consider the Egyptian letter "*f* ", the hieroglyphic character of the horned cerastes used grammatically as a *suffix pronoun* — the *Third Person Masculine Singular Pronoun* meaning, "He, Him, His."

dm sw	ḥfȝw	r	mt.n=f
Struck him	a serpent	that	died he.

I think at the very beginning, the hummingbird sought to find within *himself* the secret elixir borne by the Holy One. He prayed to the horned cerastes, that is, he looked to *himself*.

And when he learned that he did not possess the means to do this thing, but that it required becoming a new flower, to experience a new birth, to be "born again" — it took the wind right out of his purple sails.

He flew off and returned to his former ways and ignored the Wisdom of the Uræus serpent.

And shortly thereafter, a serpent struck him and he died.

Interpreting the symbol of the cerastes, I believe he self-destructed.

Why?

Because his desire to obtain the poison of eld was actually an expression of his Pure Will. But like Simple Simon, he was unwilling to pay the price. He was at odds with his own Pure Will, and it rent him asunder.

The Ibis

55. But an Ibis that meditated upon the bank of Nile the beautiful god listened and heard.

Here, we now come to the beautiful moral of this story. An Ibis meditating upon the bank of the Nile listened to the conversation between the sacred Uræus and the hummingbird.

First, we need to remember that the Ibis was sacred to *Thoth*, the god of Magic, Writing and Wisdom.

Here, the Ibis signifies divinely inspired Wisdom.

He meditated upon the bank of the river Nile.

The Egyptian word for "Nile" was ![glyph], *ḥꜥpy,* "hapy." Note that Liber LXV says, "Nile the beautiful god," which at first, may seem to be a strange phrase. In actuality, it is a perfectly accurate phrase because the Nile was personified as the god ![glyph], *ḥꜥpy,* whose name signified the divine form of that word.[45]

---

45   *Wb*, III, p. 42.

The Egyptians called the annual flooding of the Nile, "the arrival of Hapy."⁴⁶ The annual flooding encompassed Upper and Lower Egypt, thus he was often depicted in a dual form as "Hapy of the South" and "Hapy of the North."⁴⁷

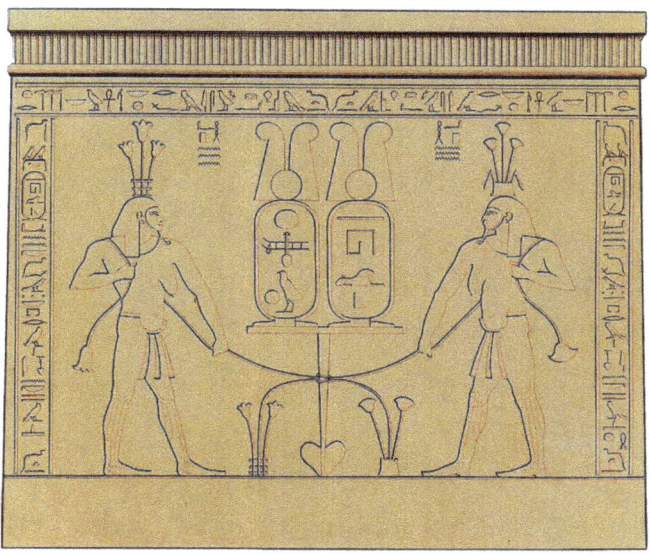

55. But an Ibis that meditated upon the bank of Nile the beautiful god listened and heard. And he laid aside his Ibis ways, and became as a serpent, saying Peradventure in an hundred millions of millions of generations of my

---

46   Wilkinson, *The Complete Gods and Goddessess of Ancient Egypt*, p.106.

47   ![glyph], *ḥʿpy-rsy,* "Hapy of the South", ![glyph], *ḥʿpy-mḥyt,* "Hapy of the North." (Lanzone, *Dizionario di Mitologia*, Vol. 3, Tav.198)

children, they shall attain to a drop of the poison of the fang of the Exalted One.
56. And behold! ere the moon waxed thrice he became an Uræus serpent, and the poison of the fang was established in him and his seed even for ever and for ever.

Most importantly — the Ibis not only listened, he *heard*.

He took the words of the Uræus to heart. And the Parable suggests to us that he did not waste any time — he laid aside his Ibis ways and began *immediately* to try to become even as a serpent.

Now, note this carefully — the Ibis did this without lust of result.

He acted selflessly, praying only that perhaps in millions of years, his children's children's children — his great-grandchildren — might inherit a mere *drop* of the Holy Elixir.

You see, he willingly entered the stream of generation in the Path of Service.

And without lusting for it, he was granted the Great Reward thereby.

My friends, I speak to you of the Path of A∴A∴. We do not seek attainment for ourselves, but for those who follow us — peradventure in a thousand years, or peradventure in ten thousand years — that the host of humankind will be uplifted to new heights of awareness.

In the A∴A∴ we are not allowed to keep our attainment for ourselves.

Any attainments granted are *always* the inheritance of those who follow us.

I am so fortunate because I have been privileged to stand on the shoulders of giants, the Masters who went before me, who taught me, who suffered my childish actions and inactions, who waited patiently for me to grow up a little, who made it possible for me, *even me*, to fashion the Infinite from a *pale* image of fine Gold.

And what did they ask from me?

Do even as we do.

Anyone who seeks the A∴ A∴ for selfish reasons will have one of two possible outcomes.

They will either discover *selflessness* in themselves and begin to work to serve humankind, or they will *fail*.

Now we see our wise Ibis, setting aside his habitual ways, selflessly stepping into the stream of generation, praying that his actions might someday find one of his offspring laying their hand upon God.

And Lo!

Before the moon waxed three times, the poison of the fang was established in *him* and his *seed*, for ever and for ever.

The Ibis did not offer Faith. He did not offer "Lip Service."

He offered Service.

I was taught some fifty years ago that any habit we want to break, or any new habit we hope to establish, takes a minimum of *three months*. The Moon must wax and wane three times before you can realize success.[48]

What does that tell us about the moral of this Parable?

The Ibis began his practice of being a serpent, and it took three months before the change had been thoroughly wrought in him.

---

48   "…in a certain aspect of psychic life, totality is symbolically expressed by three and not by four. This aspect is the developmental, temporal process of realization. Although the goal is fourfold, the process of realizing it is threefold. Thus the three and the four would represent two separate aspects of life. Four is structural wholeness, completion – something static and eternal. Three on the other hand represents the totality of the cycle of growth and dynamic change …" (Edinger, *Ego and Archetype*, p. 188.) This is another formulation of the Dialectic of Motion in its threefold aspect of Thesis-Antithesis-Synthesis. See Gunther, *Initiation in the Aeon of the Child*, pp. 160-163.

One Trimester.

Archetypally, we know that Three is the number of divinity.[49]

So who do you want to be like?

The hummingbird, still darting from flower to flower, wanting to taste the wares without paying the price? Who will you be when death overtakes you?

I don't know about you, but I have always wanted to be like the Ibis and try my best to become even as the royal Uræus serpent.

My hope has always been that some day, some sincere seeker will read my humble words and be uplifted thereby. Some day, I pray that lessons I have taught my Students will bear fruit, and that fruit will bear fruit upon fruit, so that a precious few among them may, in their turn, speak from the Invisible Throne, that their words might illumine the worlds.

I tend the garden, but I shall not see the reward.

It is enough.

I do not ask you to follow me. But who among you will walk with me?

I can promise you — it is a splendid journey.

I do wish all of you Godspeed.

And with this, speech has done with us for a while.

Love is the law, love under will.

---

49   See Gunther, *The Angel & The Abyss*, pp. 135-136.

IBIS RELIGIOSA.

Bibliography of Works Consulted

I. Published Editions by Aleister Crowley (including The Equinox)

Commentaries to the Holy Books and Other Papers. The Equinox IV(1) . York Beach, ME: Weiser (1996)

Magick. Book 4 , Parts I-IV. second edition revised and enlarged, ed. Hymenaeus Beta. York Beach, ME: Weiser (1997)

ΘΕΛΗΜΑ: The Holy Books of Thelema, The Equinox. Vol. 3, No. 9, York Beach, ME: Weiser (1988)

The Equinox. Vol. 1, No. 5. Spring (1911) Facsimile, New York: Weiser (1972)

The Equinox. Vol. 1, No. 8. Fall (1912) Facsimile, New York: Weiser (1972)

The Vision & The Voice with Commentary and other papers. The Equinox IV(2). York Beach, ME: Weiser (1998)

II. General Works

Allen, James P. *A Grammar of the Ancient Egyptian Pyramid Texts. Vol I: Unis.* Winona Lake, IN: Eisenbrauns (2017)

_____. *Ancient Egyptian Phonology.* Cambridge: Cambridge University Press (2020)

_____. *A New Concordance of the Pyramid Texts.* Vol. 1. Providence, RI: Brown University (2013)

_____. *Middle Egyptian. An Introduction to the Language and Culture of Hieroglyphs.* Cambridge: Cambridge University Press (2007)

_____. *The Debate between a Man and His Soul: A Masterpiece of Egyptian Literature.* Leiden: Brill (2011)

Allen, Thomas W. and E. E. Sikes. *The Homeric Hymns, edited with Preface, Apparatus Criticus, Notes and Appendices.* London: Macmillan and Co. (1904)

Anderson, John. *Zoology of Egypt: Volume First. Reptilia and Batrachia.* London: Bernard Quaritch (1898)

Ahlstrom, Sydney E. *A Religious History of the American People. Second Edition.* New Haven: Yale University Press (2004)

Baker, Robert. *Cicero's Three Books Touching the Nature of the Gods, done into English; with Notes and Illustrations.* London (1683)

Bartlett, William Henry. *The Nile Boat, or Glimpses of the Land of Egypt.* London: Arthur Hill, Virtue, and Co. (1849)

Bauer, Walter. *A Greek-English Lexicon of the New Testament and Other Early Christian Literature.*, trans. William F. Arndt and F. Wilbur Gingrich. Second edition revised and augmented. Chicago: Univ. of Chicago Press (1979)

Bekker, Immanuel. *Apollodori Bibliotheca.* Leipzig: Teubner (1854)

Betz, Hans Dieter. *The Greek Magical Papyri in Translation including the Demotic Spells.* Chicago: University of Chicago Press (1986)

Birdsall, Richard D. *The Second Great Awakening and the New England Social Order.* Cambridge: Cambridge University Press (1970)

Bree, C. R. *A History of the Birds of Europe, Not Observed In The British Isles.* Vol. 4. London: Groombridge and Sons (1863)

Bricault, Laurent. *Isis Pelagia: Images, Names and Cults of a Goddess of the Seas.* Leiden: Brill (2020)

Brooks, Francis. *Marci Tulli Ciceronis, De Natura Deorum.* London: Methuen & Co. (1896)

Brugsch, Henri. *Dictionnaire Hiéroglyphique et Démotique.* Vol. 2. Leipzig: J. C. Hinrichs (1868)

Budge, E. A. Wallis. *An Egyptian Hieroglyphic Dictionary.* 2 vols. London: John Murray (1920)

_____. *A Hieroglyphic Vocabulary to the Theban Recension of The Book of the Dead, Books on Egypt and Chaldea*, Vol. 31. New edition. Revised and Enlarged. London: Kegan Paul, Trench, Trübner & Co. Ltd. (1911)

_____. *The Book of the Dead, Facsimile of the Papyrus of Ani in the British Museum.* London: Longmans & Co. (1894)

_____. *The Book of the Dead, Facsimiles of the Papyri of Hunefer, Anhai, Kerasher and Netchemet.* London: Kegan Paul, Trench, Trübner & Co. (1899)

_____. *The Book of the Dead, The Chapters of Coming Forth by Day.* Vol. 1, *The Egyptian Text in Hieroglyphic* & Vol. 3, *A Vocabulary in Hieroglyphic to the Theban Rescension of The Book of the Dead.* London: Kegan Paul, Trench, Trübner & Co. (1898)

_____. *The Book of the Dead. The Papyrus of Ani in the British Museum.* Second Edition. Kegan Paul, Trench, Trübner & Co. (1894)

_____. *The Gods of the Egyptians; or, Studies in Egyptian Mythology.* 2 vols. London: Methuen & Co. (1904)

Burnet, John. *Platonis Opera: Recognovit Brevique Adnotatione Critica Instruxit* Vol. II. Oxford (1810)

Çerny, J. *Coptic Etymological Dictionary.* Cambridge: Cambridge University Press (1976)

Chadwick, John. *The Mycenaean World.* Cambridge: Cambridge University Press (1976)

Champollion, Jean-Francois. *Panthéon Égyptien: Collection des personnages mythologiques de l'ancienne Égypte.* Paris: Firmin Didot (1823)

Cochran, Doris M. *Poisonous Reptiles of the Word: A Wartime Handbook.* Washington, DC: The Smithsonian Institution (1943)

Cory, Charles B. *The Beautiful and Curious Birds of the World.* Boston: Published by the Author (1883)

Crum, W. E. *A Coptic Dictionary.* London: Oxford University Press (1979)

D'Orbigny, Charles M. *Dictionnaire universel d'historie naturelle.* Vol. 2, Atlas. Paris: Renard-Martinet (1847)

Denslow, W. W. *Denslow's Mother Goose.* New York: McClure, Phillips & Company (1901)

Department of Defense. *Venomous Snakes of the Middle East (Identification Guide), DST-1810S-469-91.* Frederick, MD (1991)

Department of the Navy Bureau of Medicine and Surgery. *Poisonous Snakes of the World. A Manual for use by U.S. Amphibious Forces (Navmed P-5099).* Washington D.C. (1965)

Dindorf, Karl Wilhelm. *ΣΟΦΟΚΛΟΥΣ ΑΝΤΙΓΙΟΝΗ*, *Sophoclis Antigone*. Leipzig: Teubner (1873)

Dindorf, Ludwig. *ΕΥΡΙΠΙΔΗΣ*, *Euripidis Opera Omnia*. 2 Vols. Oxford: J. H . Parker (1891)

_____. *ΞΕΝΟΦΩΝΤΟΣ ΕΛΛΗΝΙΚΑ*, *Xenophontis Historia Graeca*. Leipzig: Teubner (1824)

D'ooge, Martin L. *Sophocles' Antigone*. Boston: Ginn, Heath & Co. (1884)

Downes, William Howe. *The Life and Works of Winslow Homer*. Boston: Houghton Mifflin Company (1911)

Edinger, Edward. *Ego and Archetype. Individuation and the Religious Function of the Psyche*. New York: G. P. Putnam's Sons (1972)

Edwards, Amelia B. *A Thousand Miles Up The Nile*. London: George Routledge and Sons, Ltd. (1888)

The Egyptian Book of the Dead, the Book of Going Forth by Day, Twentieth Anniversary Edition, revised and expanded. trans. R.O. Faulkner & Ogden Goelet, Jr., with *A Survey of Egyptian Scholarship* by J. Daniel Gunther. San Francisco: Chronicle Books (2015)

Emlyn-Jones, Chris and William Preddy. *Plato: Euthyphro, Apology, Crito, Phaedo*. Cambridge: Harvard University Press (2017)

Erichsen, W. *Demotisches Glossar*. Copenhagen: Ejnar Munksgaard (1954)

Erman, Adolf. *Aegypten und Aegyptisches Leben im Altertum*. Tübingen: Lauppschen Buchhandlung (1885)

_____. *Aetyptisches Glossar*. Berlin: Reuther & Reichard (1904)

_____. *Life in Ancient Egypt*. (trans. H. M. Tirard). London: Macmillan & Co. (1894)

Erman, Adolf and Hermann Grapow. *Wörterbuch der Aegyptischen Sprache*. 7 Vols. Leipzig/Berlin (1950-1971)

The Encyclopedia Britannica. 30 Vols. New York: The Werner Company (1902)

Faulkner, Raymond. *A Concise Dictionary of Middle Egyptian*. Oxford: Griffith Institute (1962)

_____ (trans.) *Berlin Papyrus 3024* under the title, *The Man Who Was Tired of Life* in *The Journal of Egyptian Archaeology*, Vol. 42, pp. 21-40 (1956)

Faulkner, Raymond and Boris Jegorovic. *A Concise Dictionary of Middle Egyptian, Modernized* by Boris Jegorovicv. Available at www.egyptologyarchive.com.

Fowler, H. N. *Plato with an English Translation, Vol. 6, Cratylus*. London: William Heinemann (1926)

Frankfort, Henri. *Kingship and the Gods. A Study of Ancient Near Eastern Religion as the Integration of Society & Nature*. Chicago: University of Chicago Press (1978)

Frazer, Sir James George. *Apollodorus, The Library*. Vol. 1. London: William Heinemann (1921)

Gardiner, Alan. *Ancient Egyptian Onomastica*, Vol. 2. Oxford: Oxford University Press (1947)

_____. *Egyptian Grammar. Being an Introduction to the Study of Hieroglyphs*. Third Edition. Oxford: Griffith Institute (1978)

Gilbert, Pupa & Willy Haeberli. *Physics in the Arts*. Waltham, MA: Academic Press (2012)

Glare, P.G.W (ed.) *Oxford Latin Dictionary. 2 Vols*. Oxford: Oxford University Press (2016)

Goedecke, Hans. *The Report of a Dispute Between a Man and His Ba*. Baltimore: Johns Hopkins Press (1970)

Goodwin, Charles Wycliffe. *Fragment of a Graeco-Egyptian Work upon Magic*. Cambridge: Deighton, Macmillan and Co. (1852)

Gray, Louis Herbert. (ed.) *The Mythology of All Races, Vol. I, Greek and Roman*. Boston: Marshall Jones Co. (1916)

Green, Jay P. (trans.) *The Interlinear Bible Hebrew/English*. 3 Vols. Grand Rapids, MI: Baker Book House (1976)

Griffith, F. Ll. *A Collection of Hieroglyphs, A Contribution to the History of Egyptian Writing*. London: The Egyptian Exploration Fund (1898)

Griffith, F. Ll. & Herbert Thompson. *The Demotic Magical Papyrus of London and Leiden*, Vols 1 & 3. London: H. Grevel & Co (1904)

Gunther, J. Daniel. *The Angel & The Abyss*. Lake Worth, FL: Ibis Press (2014)

_____. *Initiation in the Aeon of the Child. The Inward Journey*. Lake Worth, FL: Ibis Press (2009)

_____. *Opus Alchymicum*, second edition. Wennofer House (2018)

Hall, Manly Palmer. *The Secret Teachings Of All Ages*. Los Angeles: The Philosopical Research Society, Inc. (1971)

Hanson, Erik. *World of Hummingbirds*. Mechanicsburg, PA: Stackpole Books (2009)

Heller, Eva. *Psychologie de la couleur, effets et symboliques*. Paris: Pyramyd Publishing (2009)

Hercher, Rudolf. *Claudii Aeliani Varia Historia*. Leipzig: Teubner (1870)

Hornung, Erik (trans. David Warburton). *The Egyptian Amduat. The Book of the Hidden Chamber*. Zurich: Living Human Heritage Publications (2007)

Jackson, James Grey. *An Account of the Empire of Marocco*. London: Printed by the author (1811)

Jastrow, Marcus. *A Dictionary of the Targumim, the Talmud Bibli and Yerushalmi, and the Midrashic Literature*. 2 Vols. London: Luzac & Co. (1903)

Journal of Egyptian Egyptology, Vol. 34. London: The Egypt Exploration Society (1948)

Jebb, R.C. *Sophocles. The Plays and Fragments, with Critical Notes, Commentary, and Translation in English Prose*. Vol. 2, *The Oedipus Coloneus*. Second edition, Cambridge: Cambridge University Press (1889)

Jerram, C.S. *Euripides, Helena*. Oxford: Clarendon Press (1882)

Jones, H.S. *Pausanias Description of Greece*, Vol. IV, Book X. Cambridge: Harvard University Press (1935)

Jung, Carl (trans. R.F.C. Hull). *Archetypes of the Collective Unconscious*. Princeton, NJ: Princeton University Press (1980)

_____ (trans. R.F.C. Hull). *The Structure and Dynamics of the Psyche*. Princeton, NJ: Princeton University Press (1978)

Kane, Thomas Leiper. *Amharic-English Dictionary*. 2 Vols. Wiesbaden: Otto Harrassowitz (1990)

Keimer, L. *Notes au sujet de l'hiéroglyphe et des vipères dans l'Égypte ancienne. Études d'Égyptologie No.7, pp. 1-52.* Cairo: IFAO (1945)

Lang, Andrew. *The Homeric Hymns*. London: George Allen (1899)

Lanzone, Ridolfo Vittorio. *Dizionario di Mitologia Egizia*. Vol. 3. Torino: Doyen Brothers (1886)

Lepsius, Richard. *Denkmäler aus Ägypten und Äthiopien*. 12 Vols. Leipzig: J. C. Hinrichs'sche Buchhandlung (1849-1859)

Lévi, Éliphas. *Dogma et Rituel de la Haute Magie*. 2 Vols. Paris: Germer Baillière (1861)

_____ *La clef des grand mystères*. Paris: Germer Baillière (1861)

Lévi, Éliphas. (trans. A. E. Waite). *Transcendental Magic, Its Doctrine and Ritual* London: George Redway (1896)

Lichtheim, Miriam. *Ancient Egyptian Literature. Vol. I. The Old and Middle Kingdom*. New Haven, Ct. Yale University Press (2003)

Liddell, George H. & Scott, Robert. *A Greek-English Lexicon*. Ninth edition. Oxford: Clarendon Press (1968)

Mackail, J. W. *Select Epigrams from the Greek Anthology*. London: Longmans, Green and Co. (1906)

Mathers, S.L. *The Kabbalah Unveiled*. London: Kegan Paul, Trench, Trübner & Co. Ltd. (1907)

Mayor, Joseph B. M. *Tullii Ciceronis De Natura Deorum Libri Tres*. Vol. 2. Cambridge: Cambridge University Press (1883)

Mayr, Gerald. *Fossil Hummingbirds in the Old World - The Biologist*, Vol. 52, No.1, pp. 12-15. London: The Royal Society of Biology (2005)

Merry, W.W. and James Riddell. *Homer's Odyssey*. Vol 1, Books I-XII. Oxford: Clarendon Press (1886)

Miller, Frank Justus. *Ovid Metamorphoses*. Vol.1. Cambridge (1951)

Milton, John. *The Paradise Lost*. New York: Baker and Scribner (1851)

Molen, Rami van der. *A Hieroglyphic Dictionary of Egyptian Coffin Texts*. Leiden: Brill (2000)

Monier-Williams, Monier. *A Sanskrit-English Dictionary.* Oxford: The Clarendon Press (1960)

Morrison, J. S. with contributions by J. F. Coates. *Greek and Roman Oared Warships 399-30 B.C..* Oxford: Oxbow Books (2016)

Most, Glenn W. *Hesiod, Theogony, Works and Days, Testimonia.* Cambridge: Harvard University Press (2006)

Murray, A.T. *Homer, The Iliad.* Vol. 1. Cambridge: Harvard University Press (1946)

Naville, Édouard. *Das Aegyptische Todtenbuch der XVIII bis XX Dynastie.* 3 vols. Elibron Classics, facsimile reprint of 1886 edition. [no date]

Noble, Louis L. *The Course of Empire, Voyage and Life, and Other Pictures of Thomas Cole.* New York: Cornish, Lamport & Company (1853)

_____. *The Life and Works of Thomas Cole, N.A.* Third Edition. New York: Sheldon, Blakeman & Company (1856)

Peck, Harry Thurston. *Harper's Dictionary of Classical Literature and Antiquities.* New York: Harper & Brothers Publishers (1898)

Plaistowe, F.G. *Aristophanes: Ranae.* London: W.B. Clive (1896)

Preisendanz, Karl. *Papyri Graecae Magicae,* Vol. 1. Leipzig: Teubner (1928)

Quirke, Stephen. *Going out in Daylight, prt m hrw, the Ancient Egyptian Book of the Dead, translation, sources, meanings.* Croydon, UK: Golden House Books (2013)

Rackham, H. *Cicero in Twenty-Eight Volumes. Vol. XIX, De Natura Deorum, Academica.* Cambridge: Harvard University Press (1933)

Regardie, Israel (ed.) *777 and Other Writings of Aleister Crowley.* York Beach ME: Samuel Weiser, Inc. (1986)

Ridgway, Robert. *The Humming Birds.* Washington, DC: Government Printing Office (1892)

Roberts, David. *The Holy Land, Syria, Idumea, Arabia, Egypt and Nubia.* Vol. IV. London (1856)

Rogers, Benjamin Bickley. *Aristophanes*. Vol. 2. London: William Heinemann (1924)

Rolfe, John C. *Ammianus Marcellinus*, Vol. 1. Cambridge: Harvard University Press (1935)

Schneemann M, R. Cathomas, S. T. Laidlaw, A.M. El Nahas, R.D.G Theakston & D.A. Warrell. *Life-threatening envenoming by the Saharan horned viper (Cerastes cerastes) causing micro-angiopathic haemolysis, coagulopathy and acute renal failure: clinical cases and review*. Oxford: QJM, An International Journal Of Medicine, Vol. 97, No. 11, pp. 717–727 (November 2004)

Scholem, Gershom. *Kabbalah*. New York: Meridian Books (1978)

Sethe, Kurt. *Die Altaegyptischen Pyramidentexte nach den Papierabdrücken und Photographien des Berliner Museums*. Vol. 1 & 2. Leipzig: J.C.Hinrich'sche Buckhandlung (1908 & 1910)

Sharpe, Samuel. *The Alabaster Sarcophagus of Oimenepthah I, King of Egypt*. London: Longman, Green, Longman, Roberts and Green (1864)

Shoemann, George Frideric. *Comparatio Theogoniae Hesiodeae*. Leipzig: Weidmenn (1847)

Skeat, Walter W. *An Etymological Dictionary of the English Language*. New York: Macmillan and Co. (1882)

Smith, William. *Dictionary of Greek and Roman Biography and Mythology*, 3 Vols. London: John Murray (1880)

Spassky, Natalie. *American paintings in the Metropolitan Museum of Art. Vol. II. A Catalogue of Works by Artists born between 1816 and 1845*. New York: Metropolitan Museum of Art (1985)

Spiegelberg, Wilhelm. *Der Ägyptische Mythus Vom Sonnenauge*. Strassburg: Vorm R. Schultz & Co (1917)

_____. *Koptisches Handwörterbuch*. Heidelberg: Carl Winters Universitätsbuch-handlung (1921)

Stallbaum, Johann Gottfried. *Eustathii, Archiepiscopi Thessalonicensis Commentarii ad Homeri Iliadem*, Vol. 1. Leipzig: Weigel (1827)

_____. *Platonis Opera Omnia, Uno Volumine Comprehensa*. Leipzig: Otto Holtze (1881)

Stein, Heinrich. *Herodotos*. 3 Vols. Berlin: Weidmannsche Buchhandlung (1868-72)

Stoker, Bram. *Dracula, A Mystery Story*. New York: W. R. Caldwell & Co. (1897)

Store, F. *Sophocles*. Vol.1. London: William Heinemann (1912)

Strong, James. *Strong's Exhaustive Concordance*. Vancouver: Praise Bible Publishers, Ltd. [no date].

The New Shorter Oxford English Dictionary (ed. Lesley Brown) 2 Vols. Oxford: The Clarendon Press (1993)

Thomov, Thomas. *Four Scandinavian Ship Graffiti from Hagia Sophia*. In Byzantine and Modern Greek Studies, Vol. 38, No. 2, pp. 168-184. Cambridge: Cambridge University Press (2014)

Tregelles, Samuel Prideaux, (trans.) *Gesenius' Hebrew and Chaldee Lexicon of the Old Testament Scriptures*. Grand Rapids, MI: Baker Book House (1979)

Vycichl, Werner. *Dictionnaire étymologique de la langue Copte*. Leuven: Peeters Publishers (1983)

Waite, Arthur Edward. *The Doctrine and Literature of the Kabalah*. London: Theosophical Publishing Society (1886)

_____. *The Holy Kabbalah*. New York: Carol Publishing Group (1990)

Wescott, Brooke Foss and Fenton John Anthony Hort. *The New Testament in the Original Greek. Revised American Edition*. New York: Harper & Brothers (1891)

Whymper, Charles. *Egyptian Birds, For the Most Part Seen in The Nile Valley*. London: Adam & Charles Black (1909)

Wilkinson, J. Gardiner. *The Manners and Customs of The Ancient Egyptians. New edition revised and corrected*. 3 Vols. London: John Murray (1878)

Wilkinson, Richard W. *The Complete Gods and Goddesses of Ancient Egypt*. London: Thames & Hudson, Ltd. (2003)

Wilkinson, Toby. *The Nile. A Journey Downriver Through Egypt's Past and Present*. New York: Alfred A. Knopf (2014)

Williamson, Sheri L. *A Field Guide to Hummingbirds of North America*. New York: Houghton Mifflin Company (2001)

Wilson, Alexander and Charles Lucian Bonaparte. *American Ornithology; or the Natural History of The Birds of the United States*, Vol. 1. Edinburgh: Constable & Co. (1831)

Yonge, C. D. Cicero's *Tusculan Disputations; also, treatises on The Nature of the Gods and on The Commonwealth*. New York: Harper & Brothers (1888)

Zehl, Donald J. *Plato: Complete Works*, ed. John M. Cooper. Indianapolis: Hackett (1997)

III. Egyptian Papyri

18th Dynasty Papyrus of 𓏺𓏺𓏺 𓀀 *Nu (British Museum 10477)*

19th Dynasty Papyrus of 𓅐 𓏼 𓏭𓏭 𓀀 *Any (British Museum 10470)*

19th Dynasty Papyrus of 𓉐 𓅐 𓊃 𓀀 *Herunefer (British Museum 9901)*

19th Dynasty Papyrus of an unnamed man. (Dublin 1661)

20th Dynasty Papyrus of 𓏭𓏭 𓉐 𓅐 𓏭𓏭 𓐍 𓀀 𓃩 *Anhay (British Museum 10472)*

About the Author

J Daniel Gunther is considered one of the foremost scholar-practitioners of Thelema. He has authored several books that focus on the theology of Thelema while drawing on his extensive knowledge of Egyptology, Jungian Psychology, Qabalah, Alchemy, Gnosticism and Philosophy. He is also the artist and writer of an original work on mystical Alchemy. Gunther's overview on the history of academic research in Egyptian religion and philology is published in the 20th Anniversary Edition of the Egyptian Book of the Dead, by Chronicle Books. J. Daniel Gunther has lectured extensively worldwide and his works have been translated into multiple languages.

www.jdanielgunther.com

Published Books by J. Daniel Gunther

Initiation in the Aeon of the Child
The Inward Journey - Book I
Published by Ibis Press

The Angel and the Abyss
The Inward Journey - Books II & III
Published by Ibis Press

The Visions of the Pylons
A Magical Record of Exploration in the Starry Abode
Published by Ibis Press

Pythagoras
His Life and Teachings
As Co-editor
Published by Ibis Press

Opus Alchymicum
An Illuminated Epistle on the Philosopher's Stone
1st Deluxe Edition published by COLLECTIVE 777
2nd Deluxe Edition published by Wennofer House

The Egyptian Book of the Dead
The Complete Papyrus of Ani
Introductory essay, "Coming Forth Into the Day"
20th Anniversary Edition published by Chronicle Books.

Thelemic Lecture Series
An ongoing series of lectures on Thelema
Published by Wennofer House

Parties interested in contacting the A∴A∴
may address their correspondence to:

Chancellor
BM ANKH
London WC1N 3XX
ENGLAND

www.outercol.org

www.ingramcontent.com/pod-product-compliance
Lightning Source LLC
Chambersburg PA
CBHW070427010526
44118CB00014B/1933